Magda Guinovart
Photographs: Rafael Manchón

PAINTING ON WOOD

for Beginners

KÖNEMANN

Author: Magda Guinovart

Photographs: Rafael Manchón

Editors: Raquel Redondo, Rosa Tamarit

Project management: Arco Editorial, S.A., Barcelona

Original title: *Pintura decorativa de muebles*

ISBN 3-8331-1704-4

© 2006 for the English edition: Tandem Verlag GmbH

KÖNEMANN is a trademark and an imprint of Tandem Verlag GmbH

Translation from Spanish: Yolanda Witney in association with

Cambridge Publishing Management

Editor: Chris Murray in association with

Cambridge Publishing Management

Typesetting: Cambridge Publishing Management

Project management: Steven Carruthers for

Cambridge Publishing Management

Project coordination: Kristin Zeier

Printed in Slovenia

ISBN 3-8331-1703-6

10 9 8 7 6 5 4 3 2 1

X IX VIII VII VI V IV III II I

Contents

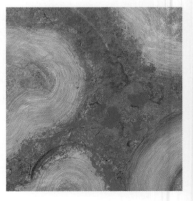

Introduction

Decorating natural materials such as wood is one of the best ways to relax and forget the stresses and strains of everyday life. By decorating furniture or any other piece of wood, we not only develop our natural creativity, but also gain unique pieces of furniture to enliven our homes.

It has to be admitted, however, that the size of certain pieces of furniture, and the apparent difficulty of the techniques of treatment and decoration, puts off some people even before they start.

This book will show even the faint-hearted that transforming a piece of furniture, and thereby enlivening the décor of your home, need not be difficult, and can also be fun.

You can in fact obtain amazing results with very simple techniques, and the resources available to add color and texture to your furniture are now very varied.

It's likely that you have already thought of a piece of furniture in your home that needs a makeover: that old chest of drawers you

inherited, or the cheap piece of furniture long forgotten at the back of your attic. Why not make them both serviceable and attractive once more? Or you could, of course, surprise your family and friends with presents decorated by you.

Have a go! Follow our instructions and you will see that all you need to obtain a unique and decorative finish is a little money and a little imagination as well as the will to try!

This book contains 30 of the most widely used techniques for

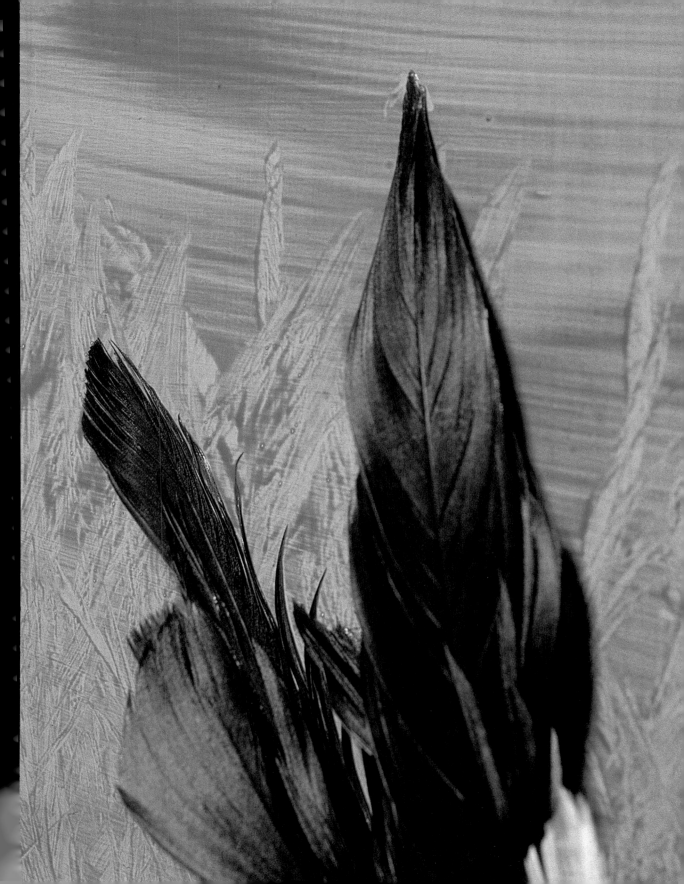

decorating wood, illustrated step by step with pictures and clear instructions.

We have applied these techniques to a wide range of furniture items, so you will be able to enjoy a simple tray or a headboard you have decorated, as well as lamp stands, tables, bookshelves, bottle racks, picture frames, trunks, coat hangers, chairs and many other items that will be of use and delight both you and your family.

Because there are so many techniques, and because more than one technique can be applied to the same piece, the techniques we have illustrated are representative rather than comprehensive. But you can of course vary the color, pattern, or finish according to your own taste or the décor in your home.

The techniques are classified in three sections according to the size of the object to be painted. Although large pieces of furniture are not necessarily more difficult to work with, you must take into account the fact that they will require a larger space to work in.

The materials and tools you'll need are readily available in hardware and do-it-yourself stores, and if used properly they are quite safe to work with.

Decorative paint techniques, and the preparation of surfaces

Wood is used extensively in furniture: in chairs, tables, chests, dressers, cupboards, larders… In the very early pieces of furniture that have survived we can observe not only the wide and skillful use of wood, but also the care taken by craftsmen to decorate them. Decorating furniture gives it charm and individuality.

Styles change, of course, and the many effects created today are often very different from those of yesteryear. The idea of treating new wood so that it has a well-used and antique look (to "distress" a piece) would have been inconceivable in another period.

Probably the main motivation for decorating wood furniture today is the desire to express our own personal taste and individuality in a world where everything seems standardized, uniform, and synthetic.

The introduction of new materials now allows us to obtain certain very distinctive effects that were originally very difficult, or even impossible.

How different the work of Renaissance artists would have been if they had had the wide range of ready-to-use paints and products that are now available in shops!

The less attractive side of recent developments, however, is that because of large-scale and indiscriminate felling, some tree species, such as ebony and rosewood, are close to extinction. Fortunately, there are now programs of conservation, especially for the slow-growing species.

And though the rare varieties themselves may not be available, decorative paint techniques can convincingly recreate the appearance of exotic, rare, and expensive woods on more common, inexpensive and easily renewed varieties of wood.

Preparation of surfaces

To obtain the best possible finish in the decoration of furniture, it's important that the surface to be painted is smooth and free from old paint, fungus, grease, and woodworm.

Although in this book we have started from scratch, and the pieces we work on have no previous paint or varnish, old pieces of furniture need to be free of paint or varnish. Fortunately, it's relatively easy to clean old pieces of furniture.

Old woods, especially those from conifers, sometimes have woodworm. It is advisable to assess the damage done by woodworm, and if it is not excessive you can apply an anti-woodworm product with a brush or spray. The holes must then be sealed with filler. Size permitting, you can also seal a piece of furniture in a large plastic bag to allow the anti-woodworm product to work for a few days.

Paint stripping

The most common way to get rid of old paint is to use chemical paint stripper. A blowtorch is not advisable as it easily leaves burn marks on the wood, nor a scraper or metallic brush (unless the paint is already loose) as the fibers of the wood can be damaged.

Paint stripper is a highly powerful substance of gelatine-like consistency that is applied to a surface in thick coats. Its consistency allows it to be worked into moldings, gaps, or cavities. Once applied, leave it for 15 minutes and then use a scraper to remove the soft paint before it dries again. Follow the manufacturer's instructions carefully (these can vary from one manufacturer to another). Don't forget to ventilate the room while you are working, and also use thick rubber gloves, protec-tive goggles, and clothes to cover your skin.

Once the paint has been removed, it is advisable to clean the surface with a cloth that has been dampened with mineral spirits; this neutralizes the effect of the paint stripper. Finally, let the wood dry.

Once an old piece of furniture has been treated in this way, you will obtain the same results as you would from a new piece of furniture that is ready to be deco-rated from scratch.

Wood filler

The next step is to fill any holes or cracks in the wood. Apply the wood filler with a plastic trowel or palette knife, leaving it proud so that it can be sanded down to the level of the wood. When it has dried completely, sand the whole piece with medium-grade sandpaper – always following the grain of the wood – and then brush away the dust.

Wood filler is normally made of a mixture of PVA glue and sawdust; once set, it can be stained or painted with a water-based paint. It's not a good idea to fill deep cracks with the wax bars that are sometimes used to fill superficial cracks; the wax, which has an oil base, will not absorb dye or any water-based paint.

Gesso

The preparation of the surface varies according to the decorative technique used. In some cases the application of gesso is required. Though both gesso and sealer are used to seal the grain of a piece of wood, a sealer is a transparent substance whereas gesso is opaque.

An excellent base for any painting technique that requires a smooth and white background, gesso has been used for centuries as a base for oil painting on wood, especially in fine art.

Traditional gesso is made with a mixture of chalk (whiting), a water-based agglutinative derived from animal skins or casein (which is obtained from dairy produce), and zinc white pigment (Chinese white).

Nowadays, a ready-to-use synthetic gesso can be bought. Made with plaster, acrylic resin, and white pigment, it is much easier to use and does not deteriorate.

Gesso is applied very thinly with a flat brush. Once it has dried, it is sanded with fine sandpaper. Two more coats of gesso (each coat has to be sanded down) provide a very smooth surface, ideal for techniques like "porcelain." Because gesso is an opaque substance, you shouldn't use it if you want to enhance the grain of the wood.

Sealers

Like gesso, these prepare a wood surface for painting by sealing it; without a sealer wood absorbs too much paint. The most widely used sealers are resins dissolved in alcohol.

They are especially good for oak, which tends to have a naturally open grain. The transparency of the sealer allows the grain of the wood to show through fully.

It's advisable to sand wood before applying the sealer. Sand again after the first coat of sealer has dried and then proceed to apply a second coat of sealer.

To make sure the sealer penetrates thoroughly, rub it into the wood with a piece of hessian cloth, using circular movements. Wipe away the excess with another cloth, always following the grain of the wood.

Materials, tools, and types of paint

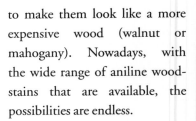

As well as sealer and gesso primer, which are used to prepare wood before painting it, the most frequent materials for painting on wood include: woodstains, waxes, varnishes, and many other products for specific techniques, paints, and paint thinners.

More lavish techniques include using silver or gold leaf, and the inlaying of mother-of-pearl.

We can now look in more detail at the materials and tools you'll need.

Materials

Woodstains

Woodstains are liquid pigments that dye wood, yet allow the grain of the wood to show through. Woodstains can be water based, oil based, or alcohol based, mixed with finely ground pigments.

The absorption of the woodstain depends on the porosity of the wood and the way the wood has been cut. The most porous woods (almond tree, birch, poplar) will take any type of woodstain, while other less porous woods will require alcohol-based tints.

In more porous parts of the wood, such as the spaces between knots and between the grain of the wood, the absorption of the tint will vary, producing a highlight effect of the grain.

Woodstains should be applied with a soaked cloth, always following the grain of the wood. Clothes must be well protected (stains are permanent) and rubber gloves must be worn. Many years ago, woodstains were used only to make light woods (pine or fir) darker and

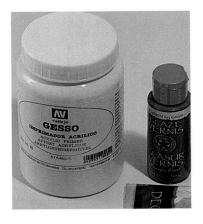

to make them look like a more expensive wood (walnut or mahogany). Nowadays, with the wide range of aniline woodstains that are available, the possibilities are endless.

As an alternative to the woodstains already mentioned, professional cabinetmakers still use the traditional chemical stains that produce a reaction and so change the actual color of the wood. One of the most widely used chemicals is potassium bichromate; when this is diluted in water it has the ability to make oak look darker and it produces a darker shade of red in light-colored mahogany.

In a similar way, a solution of crystals of potassium permanganate works on pine, producing a warm brown color.

Please remember, all chemical dyes are poisonous and so must be handled with great care.

If you are not sure of the result such chemical products will produce, it's advisable

to test them on an unseen part of a piece of furniture.

Colorings

Colorings are pigments that have been generally mixed with wax and are applied to wood with a cloth. Unlike woodstains, color- ings do not penetrate the wood fibers but adhere to the surface.

Once the wax has dried thoroughly, it can be polished by using either a soft cloth or a woollen pad.

Colorings are very easy to use but they are incompatible with certain finishes, such as polyure- thane varnish.

Decolorants

Decolorants diminish the inten- sity of color in woods. This process, traditional in Scandi- navian furniture making, is now

back in fashion because of its simple, rustic look. It can also be used to eliminate stains and clean old wood. You can use a solution of oxalic acid (1% strength), or else commercial preparations, ready to use. You must take care to add the crystals to the water and not the other way round. Given the toxicity of these preparations, you must ensure that you observe the appropriate safety precautions when you are using them.

The commercial products are a little stronger than the oxalic acid; they will tone down the natural color of the wood considerably. They come in two separate bottles and must never be mixed – if they are mixed, the chemical reaction could be very dangerous. This is how to use them: first, apply a coat of the liquid in the first bottle, and then, after a few minutes, apply the contents of the second bottle (the same quantity as the first). Decoloration is produced by a process of oxidation and must be neutralized according to the manufacturer's instructions.

Such preparations must be applied with a synthetic brush, and you must ensure that the room is well ventilated and that you are wearing suitable protection.

Waxes
Beeswax is a natural product, widely used as a finish for wood furniture: it gives it a satin sheen and a velvety touch. Wax revitalizes wood, giving it a richer color and a high-quality finish.

Apply the wax with fine steel wool, rubbing it in with wide circular movements. Then rub it well with a woollen cloth or an electric polisher; as the wax warms up, the rubbing will get easier and the characteristic shine will appear.

You can buy ready-colored wax suitable for woods like mahogany, oak, or walnut. There are also waxes containing black pigment, used to create a "distressed" or antique look.

It is advisable to seal bare wood before applying the wax.

Varnishes

Varnish is a clear paint that dries to a hard, shiny surface which protects wood from damp and wood-eating insects. Varnish usually consists of a solvent, a drying oil, and resin.

Varnishes can be classified according to their finish:

*Glossy finish, suitable for finishes like tortoiseshell effect or any other technique that requires a high sheen. It is the hardest finish, but it also shows any imperfections on the surface.

*Satin finish, the most versatile and recommended for a warm and clean look.

*Matt finish, a rather dull finish recommended for pieces of furniture that you want to have a more rustic look; a matt finish helps to hide imperfections.

The most commonly used varnishes for the decorating of wood, according to their composition, are:

Lacquer solutions to be applied by hand. This traditional method is still used by cabinetmakers and restorers to varnish valuable pieces of furniture. It is done by rubbing the surface in circular movement with a small bag, made of cloth and filled with lacquer crystals soaked in a thinner. Although it produces a fine, crystalline finish, it is not hard-wearing and the process is time-consuming. It is only recommended for antique pieces.

Oil-based varnishes consist of drying oils (like linseed oil) and hard resins. They are slow-drying, strong in odor, and tend to go yellow with time. New products, such as synthetic varnish, which are easier and cheaper to use, have largely replaced oil-based varnishes.

Polyurethane varnishes are made of polyester or acrylic resins, which provide a very durable finish. They are resistant to heat and water and can be used to seal floors and outdoor furniture. Some of the most resistant polyurethane varnishes need the addition of a catalyst.

Synthetic lacquers, which imitate the more traditional Chinese lacquer finish, consist of nitrocellulose and a plastic component. High-sheen lacquers also contain maleic resin, which will give the finish an incredibly high sheen even after the first application. They are known for their gloss and their easy application; although they are very hard, they are not recommended for floors or outdoor usage as they will crack with changes in temperature.

Natural lacquers. The best known is of Oriental origin. A

natural lacquer is made from the filtered sap of a tree, and is applied in several layers that, once dried, provide a very hard surface. Dammar varnish is a vegetable varnish that contains resins from Sumatra, and mastic is made from resins from the Greek island of Quíos. These lacquers are not very much in use any more; they are difficult to find and equally difficult to apply.

Synthetic varnishes consist of resins and drying oils diluted in hydrocarbon. Once dried, they form a very strong film resistant to the weather and to chemical agents. Colored varnishes contain a pigment; like synthetic varnishes, they are very strong (they have the same base).

Crackle medium

Crackle medium is a substance that causes a surface to crack finely so as to create the aged appearance of painted woods left outdoors. It is applied with an artist's brush over the finished surface. The quantity depends on how much cracking you want. It can be emphasized by the application of a patina.

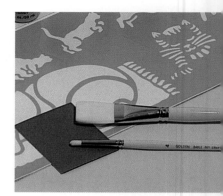

Patina

This is a dark substance used in the decoration of wood to obtain an aged or antique look. The most popular patina is asphalt, which is also used to age gold-plated objects.

You apply patina with a brush and then rub it immediately with a cloth, spreading it until you obtain the desired effect.

Liquid masking

Liquid masking is a grease-based product used to protect those areas that you don't want to cover with woodstain. It is often used to create certain very distinctive decorative effects.

Metal sheets

To carry out techniques that include gilding, you will need some sheets of gold leaves or foil. You can buy them in real gold or imitation; imitation gold is of course a lot cheaper, though the effect is very similar. Gold leaf is extremely fine and requires careful handling. Imitation or real, gold leaf is applied, with a small brush, to a coat of special gilding varnish, which acts as an adhesive.

Paints

The chemicals industry has provided an enormous variety of paints for all kinds of uses. As well as the traditional paints, gloss paints and emulsions, you can now buy anticorrosive paint, fire-resistant paint, metallic paints, non-toxic paint, bituminous paint, paint resistant to wood-eating insects, and so on.

And thanks to computerized information, many shops now offer a wide range of colors with very subtle variations of different shades, which are achieved by careful mixing.

Of course, so much choice can confuse a beginner. So we have limited ourselves to just explaining the paints we have used in the techniques shown in this book.

Acrylic paints

In nearly all the techniques we describe, acrylic paint developed for decorative use has been employed. These paints contain gouache (watercolor paint in which the pigments are bound with glue and in which the lighter tones contain an opaque white), which covers surfaces better than any normal acrylic paint. These paints are water based and therefore very easy to use, quick-drying, and odorless, and tools and brushes are easy to clean. They are ideal for nearly all the projects shown in this book.

In case a slower drying time is required, acrylic paint can be mixed with a retardant and used as if it were an oil-based paint.

Stores keep certain makes of paint with similar characteristics and in a wide range of bright colors. It's worth remembering that different manufacturers may use various different names for the same color.

With a little water and latex, acrylic paint can be used as a glaze for techniques that require a glaze.

Glaze, which adds color and depth to wood, can be bought ready to use in a thin, semi-transparent solution. The drying period of a glaze can be varied so that you can have enough time to create a specific decorative effect.

Oil paints

Oil paints consist of finely ground pigments mixed with a drying agent, usually linseed oil. When the oil dries, it forms a durable, water-resistant film that becomes

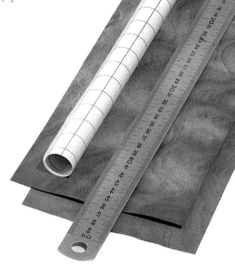

harder with time. Oil paint is more expensive than acrylic and brushes must be cleaned with mineral spirit (not water).

Because of its unequalled color, saturation, and transparency, oil paint has been widely used by artists for centuries.

The quality of acrylic paint can be equal to oil paint, but since oil paint takes longer to dry it is advisable to use it when the project requires a longer completion time.

Watercolors

Watercolors are made of finely ground pigments bound with gum arabic. They are applied with a wet brush. Whereas oil paint is well suited to strong and intense colors, watercolor can be used to create light colors which have a delicate transparency

Tools

You don't need a great many tools to perform some of the basic techniques described in this book. You probably already have some of them in your tool box or garage; if not, you can easily obtain them from a specialized hardware store or from a do-it-yourself supplier.

Some finishes require specific tools, however, such as a dragger or flogger for a streaked effect, terms and techniques that will be explained later. For tools like this, you will need to go to a specialist store.

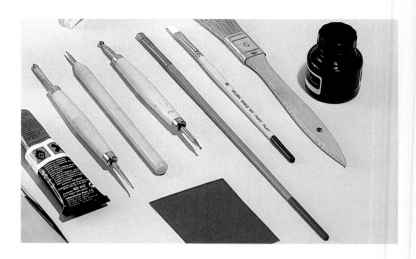

Paintbrushes

Paintbrushes are made of bristles set into a firm wood handle. They come in different sizes; flat brushes are classified according to their width and are probably the most versatile and indispensable tools when it comes to decorating furniture.

It's much better to buy good-quality brushes. If you clean them thoroughly after use they will give you a better finish and will last for many years to come. Cheap brushes come apart easily and tend to lose bristles as you paint.

If you intend to work with both oil paints and synthetic paints, it is advisable to have different kinds of brushes for each medium.

Fine-art brushes are used for precise and detailed work, and there are different types of bris-

tles, made from the fur of animals like marten or badger, as well as cheaper ones, made of synthetic fibers or other animal fur. It is advisable to have a range of brushes available when you are painting freehand.

Scrapers and palette knifes

Scrapers are used to remove old paint, and both scrapers and palette knives can be used to apply wood filler. Clean them immediately after use; dried paint, filler, or plaster on tools is difficult to remove and impairs the efficiency of a tool.

Sandpaper

If you wish to obtain a perfect finish it is essential that you rub surfaces down with sandpaper. It

comes in different grades and ranges, from very fine grain to coarse. The grade of the grain is specified at the back of the sandpaper. Fine, black-colored sandpaper, which is usually used to sand varnish, is suitable for wet surfaces and for techniques where it is important not to have dust. Brown-colored sandpaper is suitable for general use.

To use sandpaper effectively, wrap it around a block of wood or cork. As an alternative, an abrasive sponge can be used for difficult areas like grooves and corners.

If you want to use an electric sander, for example on a large piece of furniture, you must use a type of tough sandpaper especially developed for electric sanders.

You may also need a few additional special tools, including the following:

Stenciling brushes: these have short handles and compact bristles.

Dragger or flogger: a brush with long and thick bristles, which is usually made with horsehair; it is used to create a streaked effect.

Softener brush: a softener brush, usually made from marten or badger hair attached directly to a wooden handle, is used to gently spread and soften paint effects.

Comb: made of steel or rubber, this comes in different widths. It is used to drag across damp glaze to create a streaked effect.

Pyrography gun: an electric tool, similar to a soldering iron, used to burn designs into wood.

Feathers: these are used to imitate the veins in marble.

Sponges: used for the sponging technique. Synthetic sponges are very rigid, so we recommend natural sponges, which are softer and more varied in texture.

Cloths: a must, not only for cleaning and applying patina, but also for polishing wax (wool is best), and applying sealer (use hessian), or varnishing by hand (use cotton).

Steel wool: used to apply wax and to smooth varnish.

Tack cloth: used to apply color stains and certain varnishes.

Masking tape: used to define the area to be worked on and to protect the area that is to remain unpainted. It is also used to secure stencils or to keep small pieces of wood in position when being glued.

Metal ruler: this is used to take measurements and to draw straight lines.

Craft knife: used, among other things, to cut thin sheets of wood accurately, and to trim overlaps.

Engraver's chisel: available in a range of sizes, this is used to cut designs into metal sheets or wood, and also to apply gold leaf.

Screwdrivers and pliers: useful to pull out nails or screws when you have to dismantle a piece of furniture.

Drill: this enables you to drive screws through wood without splitting it; you can also attach sanding or polishing disks.

Chisel: can be used to remove glue from antique pieces so as to avoid using chemicals.

Soldering iron: used to melt wax bars and lacquer.

Press roller: used to press sheets of wood that are to be glued on to a surface.

Glue gun, stapler: needed only when a piece of furniture requires upholstery.

Transfer and tracing paper: used to trace drawings and then transfer them onto the surface to be decorated.

Rubber gloves: protects hands when applying stains or tints or using abrasive products, such as strippers.

Masks: must be used when sanding wood, especially if the dust contains metallic particles.

Cloths, plastic sheets, newspaper: used to protect furniture from dust and floors from paint splashes.

Jars and pots of various sizes: used as containers for the paint, glaze, or varnish you are using.

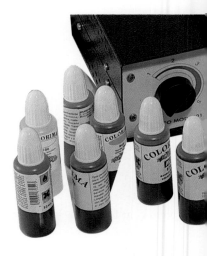

It is better to use metal containers for oil-based products.

Stirring sticks: old spoons and sticks can be used to stir and mix paint or any other products.

Techniques

The following very varied techniques will allow you to transform your furniture. They will be described in more detail in the Step-by-Step sections.

Some of the techniques have been used for centuries, others are of more recent origin. It's up to you where to start.

In some of the projects described, the surfaces will be partially or totally covered by other materials – techniques such as veneering, marquetry, or gilding create luxurious and highly decorative finishes.

Découpage, by comparison, is one of the cheapest techniques as the material used is simply paper: photographs, pictures from magazines, stamps, photocopies … anything, as long as it is in keeping with the style you wish to create.

In some techniques, stencils or printing blocks are used. These are particularly useful when the

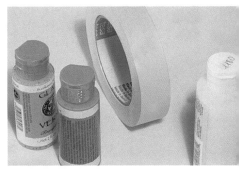

same motif has to be repeated continuously – or when the idea of drawing freehand is rather daunting, which is probably the case with the majority of beginners. Nevertheless, you don't need to be a great artist to do any of the projects in the book.

One simple trick when you need to reproduce a motif is to draw it on tracing paper, which you then place over a sheet of transfer paper; redrawing the outline on the tracing paper now transfers the design to the surface to be painted. This simple technique can be used in many decorative projects, for example pyrography.

In other projects, we have described classic techniques that transform cheap woods to make them look like more expensive ones, using techniques that imitate marble, porcelain, or oak-root grain.

Older techniques are also mentioned, including painting in the Italian or Central European style, and also painting with vinegar.

As a contrast to all these techniques, which were originally used to improve the look of old pieces of furniture, nowadays there are techniques to make new furniture look old or antique by using methods such as distressing, crackle, patina, etc.

Finally, you will also find techniques in which you have to use special tools or materials to produce a textured finish, such as combing, sponging, or flogging.

All these finishes can be executed in multiple combinations – try experimenting and be adventurous!

STEP B

Y STEP

Small furniture

Veneer

STEP BY STEP

VENEER ALLOWS YOU TO GIVE A PIECE OF FURNITURE A TOTALLY DIFFERENT APPEARANCE. WITH JUST A LITTLE APPLICATION, YOU CAN ACHIEVE AMAZING RESULTS.

VENEER MUST BE HANDLED WITH CARE AND SURFACES MUST BE PERFECT – ANY INDENTATION COULD DAMAGE THE VENEER OR ALLOW SMALL CRACKS TO APPEAR AT THE SLIGHTEST PRESSURE.

You will need:
Adhesive paper, African rosewood (bubinga) veneer, ruler, tack cloth, steel wool, glue, flat brush (No. 6), sandpaper, craft knife, pen, scraper, roller, tint in rosewood color, linseed oil, and polyurethane varnish.

Photograph 1. This shows a wooden picture frame ready to veneer.

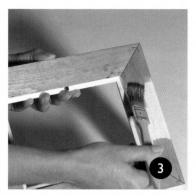

Photograph 3. With a brush apply the rosewood-colored tint to the back and sides of the frame: the veneer will cover the front.

Photograph 4. Before it dries, wipe off the excess tint with a cloth.

Photograph 2. Smooth the whole frame with sandpaper.

Photograph 5. Apply a second coat of tint and wipe away the excess.

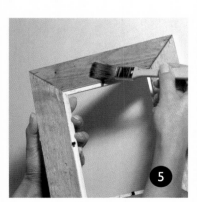

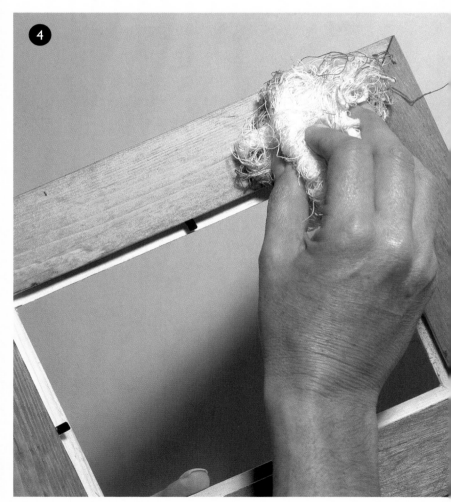

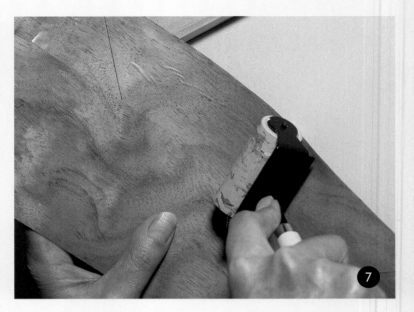

Photograph 6. With the help of transparent adhesive paper, trace out the shape of one of the sides of the frame.

Photograph 7. Stick the adhesive paper to the bubinga veneer with the help of a roller.

Photograph 8. Using a craft knife and ruler, cut out the veneer.

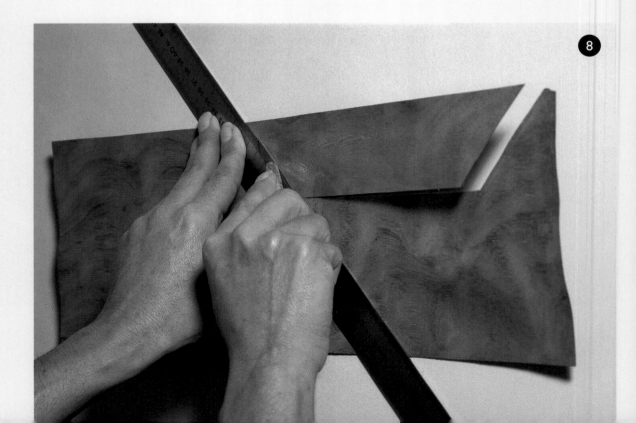

Photograph 9. With a scraper, spread glue over the back of the veneer and also on the areas of the frame to which the veneer will be glued.

Photograph 10. Put the cut veneer over the frame and press down, peeling off the clear adhesive paper at the same time. You can press the veneer down with the help of a roller.

Photograph 11. Follow the same instructions for the other three sides of the frame. Once finished, apply linseed oil to the entire surface.

Photograph 12. Wipe off the excess oil with a clean cloth.

Photograph 13. Once the oil has dried, varnish the frame with a satin varnish and leave to dry.

Photograph 14. Smooth the varnish with steel wool. Repeat the process again three times (varnish and rub with steel wool).

Photograph 15. This is the finished look of the frame. It is elegant and will set off your favorite photographs to great effect.

2

Découpage

STEP BY STEP

You will need:
Flat brush (No. 6), artist's brush, stencil brush, scissors, dragger or flogger, sandpaper, stencil, gesso, PVA glue, polyurethane varnish, and acrylic paints (yellow, orange, and dark green).

TOWARDS THE MIDDLE OF THE 17TH CENTURY, THE USE OF CUT-OUT PAPER MOTIFS WAS CONSIDERED A FORM OF ART, ALTHOUGH IT WAS NOT GENUINE DÉCOUPAGE AS LACQUER WAS NOT USED FOR THE FINISH.

THANKS TO THE WIDE RANGE OF LACQUERS AVAILABLE THESE DAYS, THIS TECHNIQUE IS BACK IN FASHION AND THE FINISH IS VERY AESTHETIC. CHOOSE MOTIFS THAT MATCH THE MATERIAL AND THE COLOR OF THE PIECE YOU ARE GOING TO DECORATE. BY COMBINING DÉCOUPAGE WITH OTHER TECHNIQUES, YOU WILL OBTAIN SUPERB RESULTS.

A view of the tray that we decorated with the découpage technique. This view allows us to see the design, the painted areas, the colors, etc.

Photograph 2. Apply the gesso to the whole surface of the tray.

Photograph 3. Sand the entire surface.

Photograph 1. The bare wood tray.

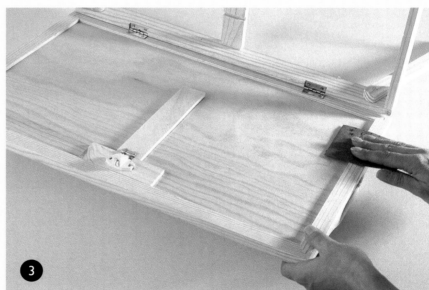

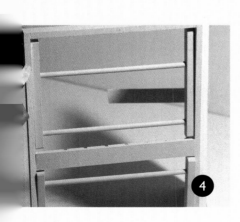

Photograph 4. With a brush, apply the yellow paint.

Photograph 5. With a brush impregnated with translucent orange, paint a swirling pattern or circles over the base of the tray.

Photograph 6. Cut out the motif you want to use and place it on the middle of the tray.

Photograph 7. Stick the motif to the tray with PVA glue. Press and rub firmly, carefully removing any air pockets or wrinkles. The pattern created with the orange paint will act as a frame.

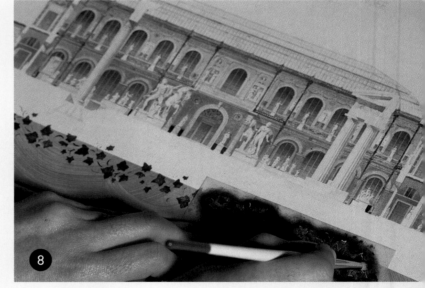

Photograph 8. To hide the cut-out line of the motif, a stenciled border of ivy leaves is superimposed around it.

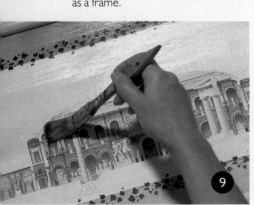

Photograph 9. Varnish the base of the tray eight times, making sure that each coat of varnish dries completely before applying the next. After the second coat of varnish, smooth each coat with sandpaper.

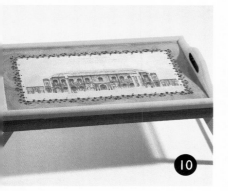

Photograph 10. General view of the finished tray decorated with the découpage technique.

Photograph 11. Close-up of the motif used to decorate the base of the tray.

Photograph 12. Here you can see one of the uses we can give this finished tray: as a book rest.

3

STEP BY STEP

Marquetry

You will need:

A selection of veneer sheets in different woods, glue, green and white mother-of-pearl, pencil, pen, craft knife, roller, spatula, Gold Sable flat brush (No. 6), mahogany tint, poly-urethane varnish, adhesive tape, carbon-copy paper, tracing paper, tack cloth, toothpick, sandpaper, acrylic colors (white and green).

MARQUETRY IS GENERALLY THOUGHT TO BE A JOB FOR THE PROFESSIONAL CABINET-MAKER, BUT IN FACT IT CAN BE DONE BY ANYBODY WHEN DECORATING A PIECE OF FURNITURE WITH DIFFERENT WOOD VENEERS. A SIMPLE PIECE OF FURNITURE MADE FROM CHIPBOARD CAN BE MADE TO LOOK LIKE SOLID WOOD BY USING THIS TECHNIQUE. GIVEN THE COMPLEXITY OF THE TECHNIQUE, WE WILL USE FLAT SURFACES – SURFACES WITH ANY KIND OF RELIEF WOULD BE ALMOST IMPOSSIBLE TO WORK WITH. THE VENEERS ARE VERY FRAGILE SO THE DESIGN MUST NOT BE TOO COMPLICATED AS VENEERS TEND TO BREAK, IF THEY ARE INTRICATE, WHEN DESIGNS ARE CUT OUT. FLOWERS OR ARABESQUES ARE THE MOST COMMONLY USED MOTIFS.

The finished sewing box decorated with marquetry.

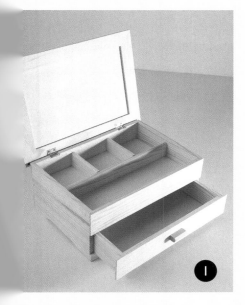

Photograph 1. General view of the sewing box and its compartments.

Photograph 2. With a piece of sand-paper, smooth down the entire surface well.

Photograph 3. Now stain the interior of the sewing box and the frame of the lid with cherry color.

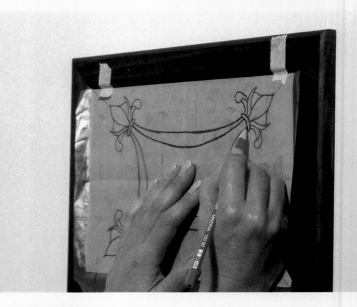

Photograph 4. Use a cloth to wipe off any excess tint before it dries.

Photograph 5. Trace the chosen design on tracing paper, then transfer the pattern to the lid of the box, securing it with tape to avoid movement. Do the same to the sides of the box.

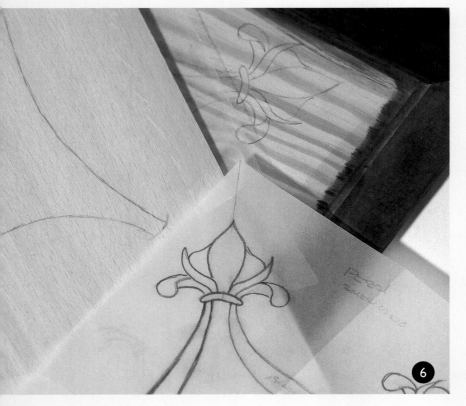

Photograph 6. Transfer part of the design to a sheet of sycamore veneer.

Photograph 7. Using a craft knife, cut out the design.

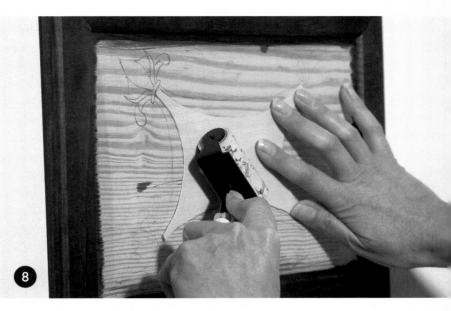

Photograph 8. Stick the piece you have just cut out onto the box, making sure you put glue on both the lid and the wood, and press with a roller to expel air bubbles.

Photograph 9. Paint in green the areas where the green mother-of-pearl is to be inserted. This will enhance its color.

Photograph 10. Apply gloss varnish over the green paint with a toothpick to avoid going over the lines of the design.

Photograph 11. Again using a toothpick, position the mother-of-pearl sections, white and green, which will stick because of the varnish.

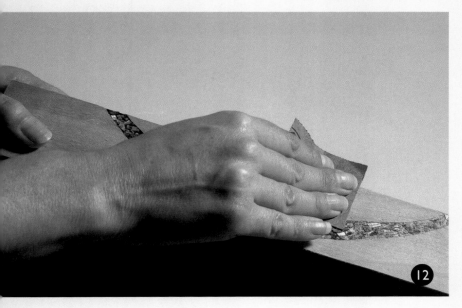

Photograph 12. Once it has dried thoroughly, sand the surface where you have just worked.

Photograph 13. Apply the first coat of polyurethane varnish to the entire piece. Once the varnish has dried, sand the whole box. Repeat this operation three or four times until you get the desired finish.

Photograph 14. In this photograph a detail of the sewing box is shown.

Photograph 15. The finished sewing box after the marquetry technique has been applied.

4

Combing

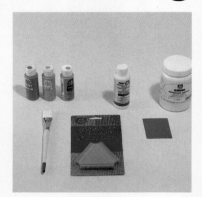

You will need:
Sandpaper, Gold Sable brush, gesso, comb, acrylic varnish, and acrylic paints (yellow, green, violet, and pink).

STEP BY STEP

THIS TECHNIQUE, WHICH WAS ORIGINALLY USED FOR WALLS, HAS RECENTLY BEEN ADAPTED FOR FURNITURE. IT CONSISTS OF REMOVING THE LAST COAT OF GLAZE OR VARNISH WITH A COMB, A PROCESS THAT CREATES A REGULAR PATTERN OVER THE SURFACE OF A PIECE OF FURNITURE. THE FINISHED LOOK DEPENDS ON HOW WIDE THE TEETH OF THE COMB ARE. THE DIREC-TION OF THE LINES IS UP TO YOU BUT VERTICAL COMBING IS THE MOST COMMON TECHNIQUE. IT'S A GOOD IDEA TO EXPERIMENT WITH DIFFERENT FINISHES. FOR A CHECKERED EFFECT, COMB ALL THE SURFACES FIRST VERTICALLY, THEN HORIZONTALLY. YOU CAN WRAP A PIECE OF LINT-FREE CLOTH AROUND THE COMB FOR A MORE PROMINENT PATTERN.

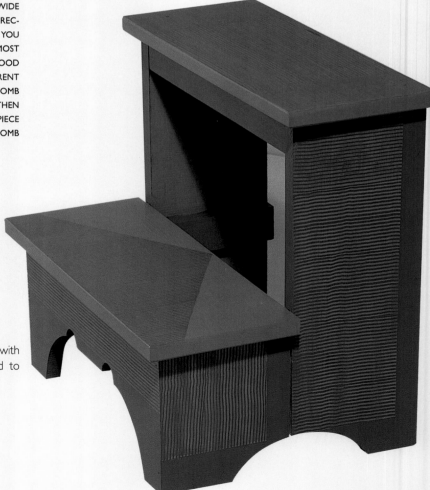

This shows the designs created with the comb technique when used to decorate a pair of low steps.

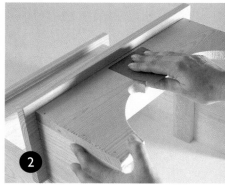

Photograph 1. The wooden steps before work begins.

Photograph 2. Prepare the surface by smoothing it with sandpaper.

Photograph 3. Apply a coat of gesso and let it dry. To make the surface smooth, sand it once more.

Photograph 4. Paint the steps with the green and violet paint.

Photograph 5. Apply pink glaze over the green paint, and before it dries drag the comb through it to create the desired pattern. Do the same to the areas painted in violet, but now use yellow glaze.

Photograph 6. Once everything has dried, apply the first coat of acrylic varnish; let it dry and then apply three more coats of varnish.

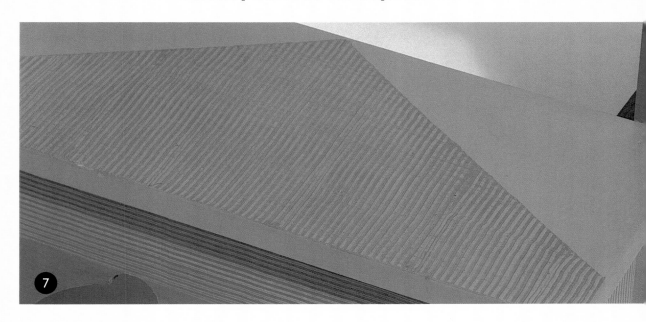

Photograph 7. Detail of the design created by combing.

Photograph 8. The finished steps once the combing technique has been applied. The bright colors are well suited to children's furniture.

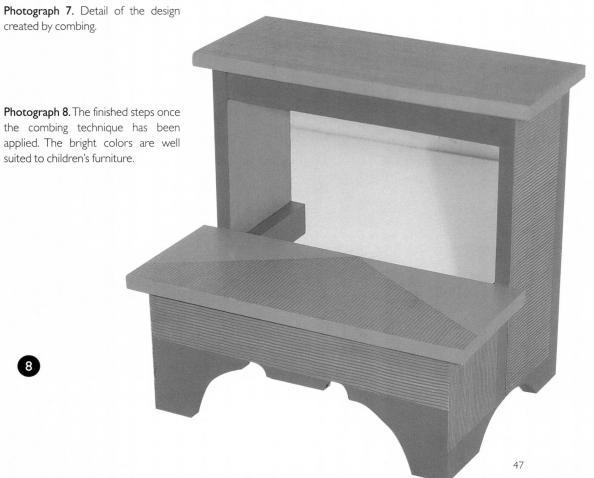

47

5 Porcelain/Crackling

STEP BY STEP

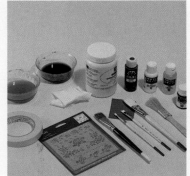

You will need:
Masking tape, plaid stencil, ox's ear brush (No. 8), stencil brush, fine flat brush, flat brush (No. 8), sandpaper, antiquing paint (asphalt), crackle medium, base for crackling, gesso, soft cloth, oak-color stain, polyurethane varnish, and acrylic color (navy blue).

A PORCELAIN EFFECT ON WOOD IS A TECHNIQUE THAT REQUIRES DETAILED WORK. IT CONSISTS OF APPLYING AS MANY COATS OF GESSO AS NECESSARY TO ACHIEVE A SURFACE SMOOTH ENOUGH TO LOOK LIKE GENUINE PORCELAIN. ONCE THIS HAS BEEN PAINTED, A CRACKLED FINISH IS ADDED TO MAKE PORCELAIN EFFECT LOOK MORE REALISTIC. WE WILL USE A VARIETY OF SPECIAL VARNISHES. WHEN YOU HAVE ACHIEVED THE EVENTUAL FINISH, YOU WON'T BE ABLE TO RECOGNIZE THE ORIGINAL PIECE OF WOOD.

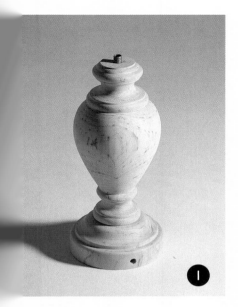

Photograph 1. The lamp before the porcelain technique.

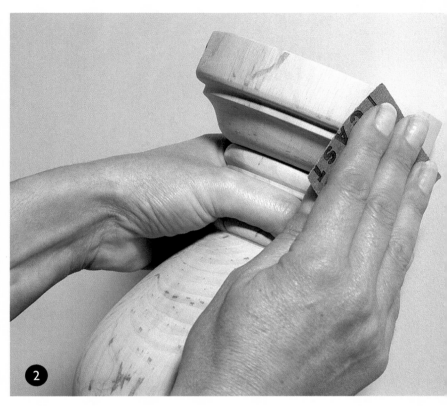

Photograph 2. First, sand the lamp to make the surface completely smooth.

Photograph 3. Stain the whole surface with oak-color stain, except for the middle part, on which the porcelain effect is to be created.

49

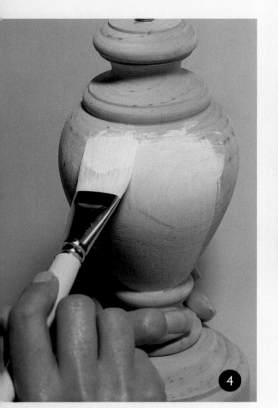

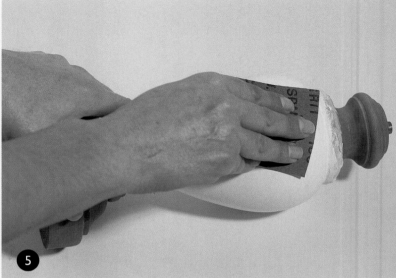

Photograph 4. Apply gesso to the area that has not been stained and let it dry.

Photograph 5. Sand the area where the gesso has been applied.

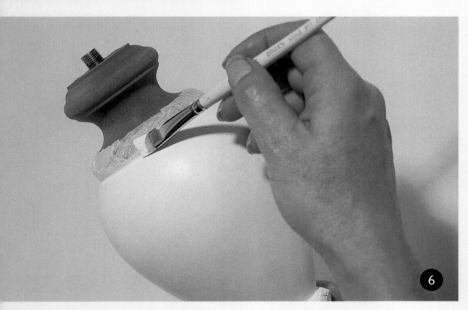

Photograph 6. Apply the gesso once more. Repeat this process two more times to obtain a totally smooth surface.

Photograph 1. Smooth down all the trays and tray holder with sandpaper.

Photograph 2. When you have decided on the design, define the lines of the design with masking tape; the aim is to cover the areas where you don't want any paint.

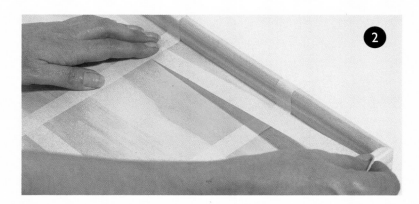

Photograph 3. Paint one of the trays with colored acrylic varnish. Repeat with the other trays.

Photograph 4. Wipe off the excess varnish with a sponge before it dries.

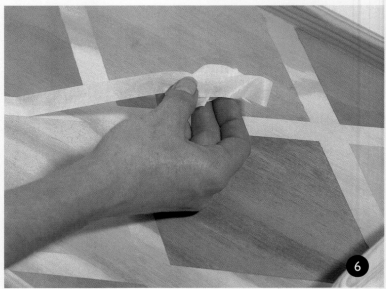

Photograph 5. Once the base is finished, remove the masking tape carefully.

Photograph 6. Once more, use the masking tape to protect the painted areas. Paint the handles and sides of the tray.

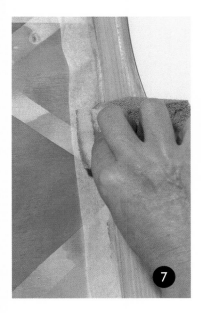

Photograph 7. Wipe off any excess paint before it dries.

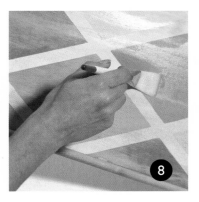

Photograph 8. When the paint has dried, apply a coat of clear polyurethane varnish. This will prevent the paint from going yellow with time.

Photograph 9. Once the polyurethane varnish has dried, apply a colored varnish around the borders of the tray.

Photograph 10. This is how the finished trays look, placed in their holder according to size.

7

Covering wood with silver foil

STEP BY STEP

THIS TECHNIQUE IS IDEAL FOR PIECES OF WOODEN FURNITURE THAT HAVE EMBOSSED OR RICHLY TEXTURED SURFACES. "DRESSING" IT WITH SILVER FOIL WILL GIVE THE PIECE A VERY ELEGANT LOOK. THE SILVER FOIL WILL EASILY GO INTO THE CREVICES AND WILL FIT LIKE A SECOND SKIN. SILVER COMBINED WITH WOOD CREATES AN ANTIQUE AND STYLISH EFFECT. THE END RESULT IS OFTEN QUITE STRIKING.

You will need:
Silver foil, adhesive, three different types of engraver's chisels, synthetic flat brush, Gold Sable brushes (Nos. 4 and 8), ink, antiquing varnish for silver, light mahogany tint, cloths, tack cloth, sandpaper, patina and polyurethane varnish.

Here we have used a mahogany chest.

Photograph 1. Sand the whole surface of the chest.

Photograph 2. To enhance the grain of the wood, apply a light mahogany stain.

Photograph 3. Wipe off the excess tint before it dries.

Photograph 4. When the tint is completely dry, apply a coat of polyurethane varnish (satin).

Photograph 5. Apply adhesive to the areas where the silver is going to be applied.

Photograph 6. Using an engraver's chisel for the details, press the silver over the wood. Try not to pierce the silver foil.

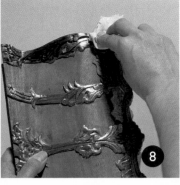

Photograph 8. Before it dries, wipe off any excess antiquing with a soft cloth.

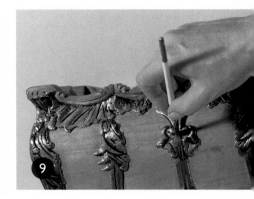

Photograph 9. Apply a coat of special varnish (to prevent the silver from tarnishing).

Photograph 7. Apply a coat of antiquing to the silver.

Photograph 10. The finished wooden chest decorated with silver foil. It will grace any home.

8 Pyrography

STEP BY STEP

You will need:

Pyrography pen, black carbon-copy paper, tracing paper, pencil, Gold Sable flat brushes (Nos. 6 and 8), sandpaper, masking tape, polyurethane varnish and yellow, dark blue, green, terracotta, red, and golden-brown watercolors.

THIS TECHNIQUE BEGAN DURING THE 19TH CENTURY, BUT IT WAS IN THE 20TH CENTURY THAT IT BECAME VERY POPULAR, THANKS LARGELY TO THE DEVELOPMENT OF AN ELECTRONIC TOOL THAT IS USED TO BURN THE DESIGNS ONTO THE WOOD. PYROGRAPHY IS USUALLY USED WITH WOOD, BUT IT CAN ALSO BE USED WITH LEATHER, GLASS, OR CRYSTAL. IF YOU HAVEN'T USED THIS TOOL BEFORE, PRACTICE ON A PIECE OF SPARE WOOD FIRST UNTIL YOU FEEL FAMILIAR WITH IT.

In this example we have used a music stand.

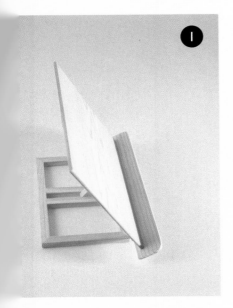

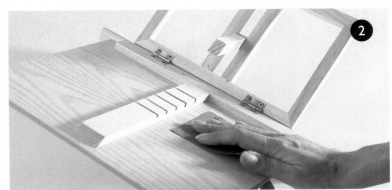

Photograph 1. The music stand before the technique was used.

Photograph 2. With some sandpaper, smooth the surface of the stand.

Photograph 3. Once you have chosen a drawing, trace it onto the stand with the carbon-copy paper. You can secure the paper with masking tape.

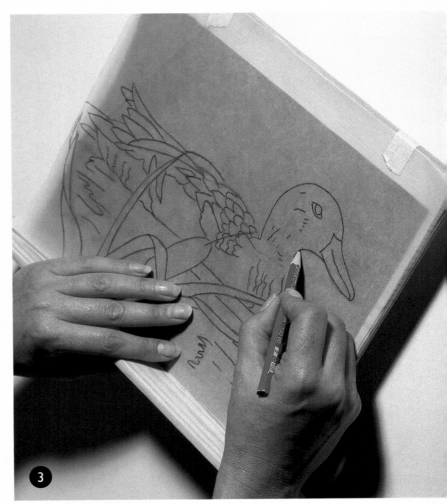

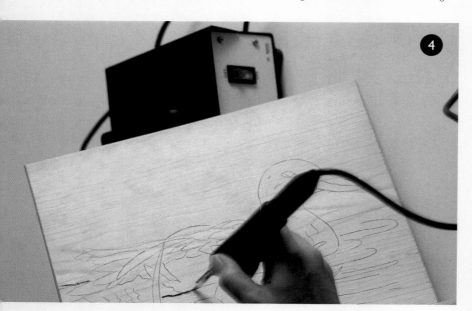

Photograph 4. With a steady hand, follow the lines of the drawing with the pyrography pen.

Photograph 5. Color the drawing with watercolors, using whatever colors take your fancy.

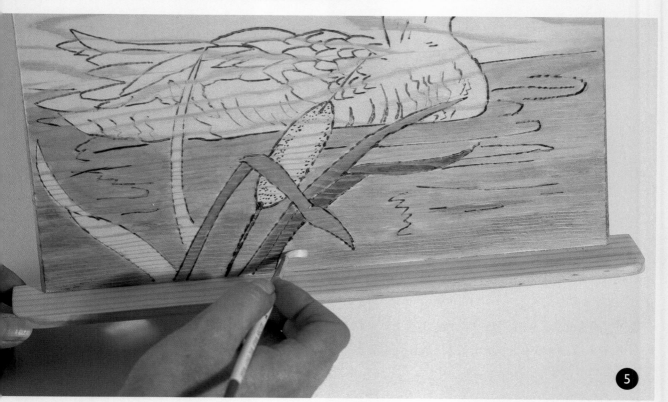

Photograph 6. When the paint has dried, apply a coat of polyurethane varnish to the entire surface of the music stand and let it dry.

Photograph 7. The finished music stand, ready to be used.

9

STEP BY STEP

Marbling

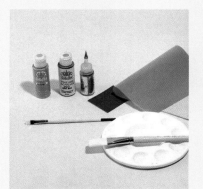

THIS TECHNIQUE IS SUITABLE FOR SMALL PIECES OF FURNITURE THAT REQUIRE A BRIGHT AND INTENSE FINISH. EFFECTIVE PATTERNS CAN BE CREATED BY USING BLACK AND WHITE GLAZE.

THERE ARE MANY KINDS OF REAL MARBLE: SOME HAVE PRONOUNCED VEINS, SOME HAVE SPECKLES, AND SOME OTHERS HAVE BOTH.

You will need:
Plastic palette or disposable paper palette, fine flat brush, Gold Sable flat brush (No. 8), tracing paper, orange carbon-copy paper, a jar for the mineral spirits, sandpaper, gesso, masking tape, acrylic varnish, and acrylic colors (salmon and gray Nos. 722 and 936 from Folkart).

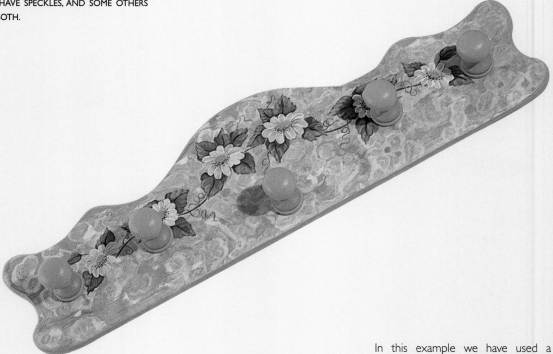

In this example we have used a coat hanger. The technique is simple but effective.

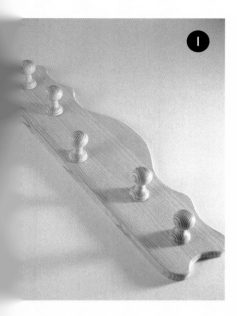

Photograph 1. The untreated coat hanger.

Photograph 2. Make the wood smooth by sanding it.

Photograph 3. Apply a coat of gesso and let it dry.

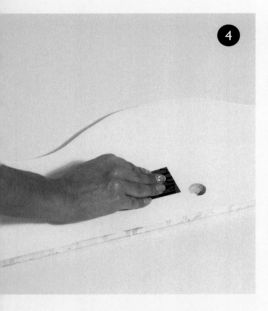

Photograph 4. Sand the gesso to obtain a smooth surface.

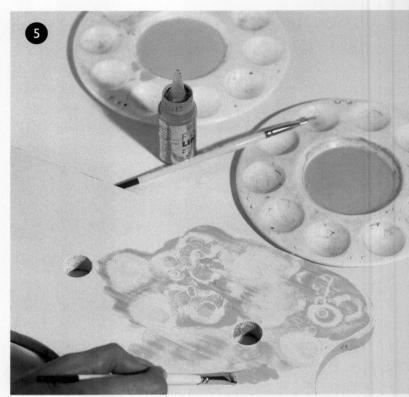

Photograph 5. Mix the salmon color with water and then the gray. Apply one of the colors first in patches and then the other, next to each other, but taking care not to apply one color on top of the other one.

Photograph 6. Before the paint dries, allow a few drops of mineral spirits to fall in the middle of the patches; this will cause the patches to expand, creating a lighter shade.

Photograph 7. Paint the edges of the coat hanger with the salmon color.

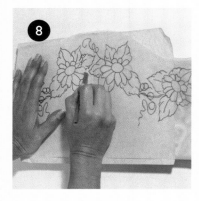

Photograph 8. Place the orange carbon-copy paper over the coat hanger, secure it with masking tape, and trace out the drawing that will decorate the front.

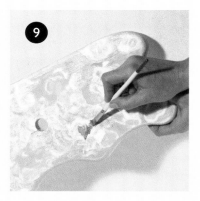

Photograph 9. Proceed to paint the drawing and allow it to dry.

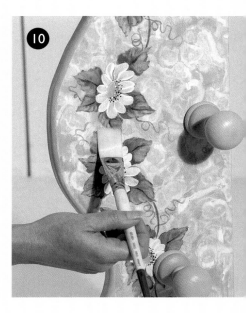

Photograph 10. Apply a coat of acrylic varnish to the entire surface and then let it dry.

Photograph 11. The finished coat hanger showing just how striking the effects created by marbling can be.

10

STEP BY STEP

Decorating with printing blocks

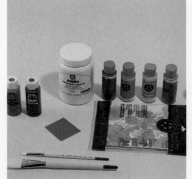

You will need:

Small flat brush, sandpaper, gesso, medium flat brush, printing blocks, acrylic varnish from Folkart, acrylic paints (red, white, and green), and green and red acrylic glaze.

PAINTING WITH PRINTING BLOCKS IS ONE OF THE MOST BASIC DECORATIVE TECHNIQUES THERE IS. IT CONSISTS OF USING A BLOCK DABBED IN PAINT TO STAMP A DESIGN ONTO A SURFACE. PRINTING BLOCKS CAN BE BOUGHT IN SHOPS OR YOU CAN IMPROVISE BY MAKING THEM FROM PIECES OF LINO, CORK, FOAM, OR ANY OTHER SUITABLE MATERIAL. YOU CAN USE THEM ON ANY TYPE OF SURFACE AS LONG AS IT IS REASONABLY FLAT AND IT ALLOWS AN EVEN ABSORPTION OF THE PAINT.

A view of the box we have used.

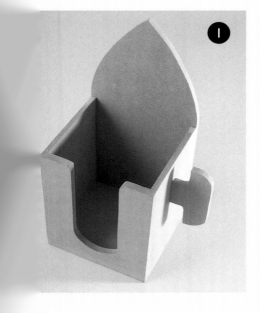

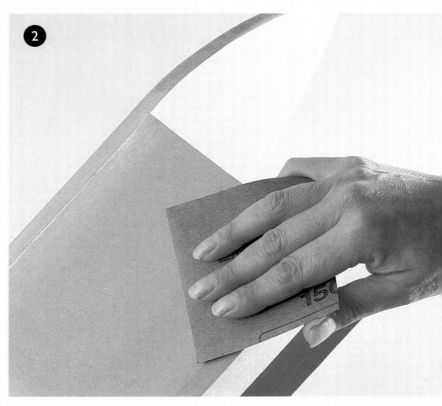

Photograph 1. The box before it is decorated.

Photograph 2. Sand down the box.

Photograph 3. Apply a coat of gesso to the whole surface.

Photograph 4. Sand down the gesso to obtain a really smooth surface.

Photograph 5. Paint the interior of the box in green.

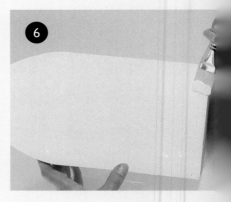

Photograph 6. Paint the exterior white. Use acrylic paints.

Photograph 7. Dip the printing block in the green or red glaze, and press it onto the surface of the box at random. With a fine brush, paint lines to represent the stalks.

Photograph 8. Paint the edge of the holder in red.

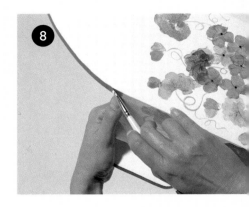

Photograph 9. Once the paint has dried, apply a coat of acrylic varnish and let it dry. Apply a second coat of varnish, and a third once the second coat has dried.

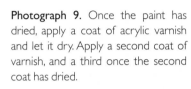

Photograph 10. A close-up of the finished box.

Stenciling

STEP BY STEP

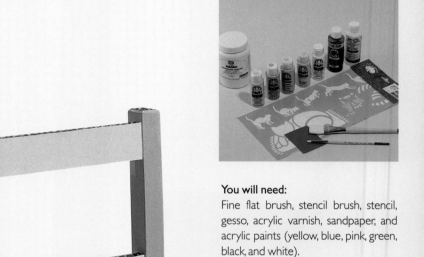

EVEN THOUGH A LITTLE PRACTICE IS NEEDED, PAINTING WITH STENCILS IS ONE OF THE EASIEST TECHNIQUES TO USE ON WOOD. IT'S ADVISABLE TO START WITH A SIMPLE DESIGN, ESPECIALLY IF THE SURFACE TO BE COVERED IS QUITE LARGE. THE STENCILS USED ARE THE SAME AS THOSE USED ON WALLS AND CAN BE BOUGHT IN A WIDE RANGE OF DESIGNS. OF COURSE YOU CAN CREATE YOUR OWN DESIGNS WITH WAXED STENCIL CARD OR ACETATE.

You will need:

Fine flat brush, stencil brush, stencil, gesso, acrylic varnish, sandpaper, and acrylic paints (yellow, blue, pink, green, black, and white).

Photograph 2. Sand the chair with sandpaper to prevent a rough finish.

Photograph 1. To illustrate this technique we have used a chair. Because it's for children, the effect will be bright and cheerful.

Photograph 3. Apply a coat of gesso to create a smoother surface.

Photograph 4. Once the gesso is dried, sand the chair again.

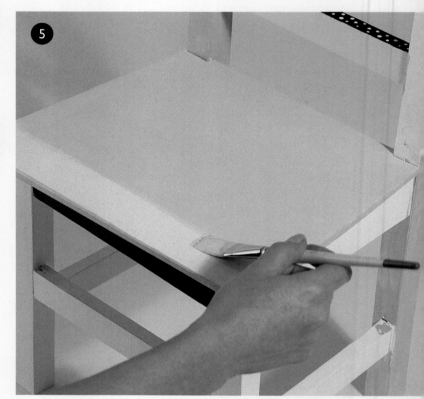

Photograph 5. Paint the chair with the base paints (pink, blue, yellow, black, and green); be adventurous.

Photograph 6. Using the tip of a brush's handle, make small white dots all over the black paint.

Photograph 7. Stencil the shape of a cat (or, of course, any other design) on the seat of the chair.

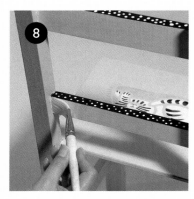

Photograph 8. When it has dried, apply a coat of acrylic varnish to the whole chair. Apply two more coats of varnish.

Photograph 9. Close-up of the cat design on the seat of the chair.

Photograph 10. The finished children's chair decorated with this attractive stencil technique.

Y STEP

Medium-sized furniture

12

STEP BY STEP

Tortoiseshell and gold leaf

You will need:
Gold leaf or foil, gesso, adhesive, antiquing, oil paints (raw sienna, Vandyke brown, black, and iron oxide red), sandpaper, gold and red acrylic paint, softener brush, soft badger brush, synthetic flat brushes (Nos. 6 and 8), fine flat brush, ox's ear flat brush (No. 5), Gold Sable flat brush (No. 9), paintbrush, gloss varnish, antiquing, paint thinner.

THE CHARACTERISTICS OF TORTOISESHELL ARE IMITATED BY MEANS OF A SERIES OF STROKES OF DIFFERENT LENGTHS AND WIDTHS APPLIED DIAGONALLY. DIFFERENT COLORS CAN BE USED: WHITE, CINNAMON, AND GOLD. TO EMPLOY THIS TECHNIQUE SUCCESSFULLY, YOU MUST CHOOSE A FAIRLY PLAIN SURFACE. IT'S NORMALLY APPLIED TO FRAMES, AND THE COLORS CAN VARY FROM VERY DARK TO VERY LIGHT.

1

Photograph 1. View of a picture frame before the technique has been applied.

Photograph 2. Sand the entire frame.

Photograph 3. Apply a coat of gesso to the surface of the frame.

Photograph 4. Once the gesso has dried, sand the frame again.

Photograph 5. Apply a second coat of gesso and sand the frame once more.

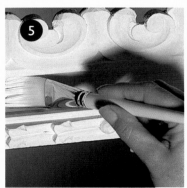

81

Photograph 6. Paint the whole frame in iron oxide red.

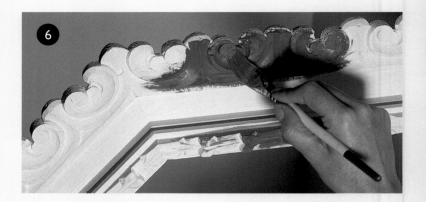

Photograph 7. Apply a coat of adhesive, being careful to get into all crevices. Let it dry until it is no longer a milky color, and then apply another coat of adhesive. Let it dry until the adhesive is clear and tacky to the touch.

Photograph 8. With a soft brush, press the foil firmly over the adhesive to make sure that the foil is firmly glued.

82

Photograph 9. With the help of a paintbrush, brush away any loose bits of foil.

Photograph 10. To protect the finish, you can apply a coat of sealer or satin varnish.

Photograph 11. Paint the edges and back of the frame with the gold paint.

Photograph 12. Apply the brown paint over the central part of the frame in small patches. This is the process that imitates tortoiseshell.

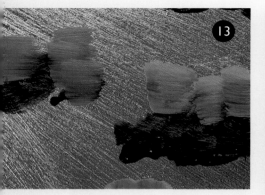

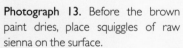

Photograph 13. Before the brown paint dries, place squiggles of raw sienna on the surface.

Photograph 14. Do the same with the red paint.

Photograph 15. Before the paints dry, draw a softener brush across them, blending them gently.

Photograph 16. With a brush soaked in brown paint and thinner, spray a few drops over the frame and let it dry for a few days.

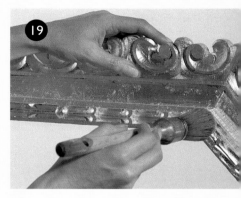

Photograph 17. Using black paint, make a line at either side of the tortoiseshell effect.

Photograph 18. Once the black paint has dried, apply a coat of gloss varnish to the tortoiseshell effect and let it dry. Repeat this operation three times.

Photograph 19. To give the frame an even older look, apply a coat of antiquing to all the parts covered with gold foil.

Photograph 20. This shows the completed picture frame.

Photograph 20a. Detail of one of the corners of the frame, where the decorative effect can be seen more clearly.

13

STEP BY STEP

St Remy marble

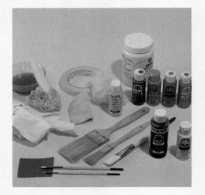

You will need:

Sandpaper, round brush (No. 3), synthetic flat brush (No. 7), fine flat brush, flogger, Gold Sable flat brush (No. 7), acrylic colors (black, white, brown, ocher, umber, iron oxide red, light gray), gesso, tack cloth, cloths, sea sponge, masking tape, a bird's feather (duck is best), and white glaze.

MARBLING IS NORMALLY USED FOR THE DECORATION OF WALLS, FLOORS, PILLARS, AND COLUMNS, BUT IT CAN ALSO BE USED TO DECORATE SMALL PIECES OF FURNITURE, SUCH AS FRAMES, BOXES, OR LAMP STANDS. ONCE THE TECHNIQUE HAS BEEN APPLIED, IT IS SEALED WITH A GLOSS OR SATIN VARNISH TO PROTECT THE SURFACE AND TO GIVE IT AN APPROPRIATE SHEEN.

THE TECHNIQUE IS QUITE FLEXIBLE AND CAN REPRODUCE A WIDE RANGE OF MARBLES. HERE WE WILL IMITATE A VERY DISTINCTIVE MARBLE, ST REMY.

We have used as an example a pedestal decorated to resemble St Remy marble.

Photograph 1. The wooden pedestal before the marbling technique has been used.

Photograph 2. Sand the entire pedestal.

Photograph 3. Apply a coat of gesso to those parts of the pedestal where the marbling technique is going to appear.

Photograph 4. Once the gesso has dried, paint those areas in light gray.

87

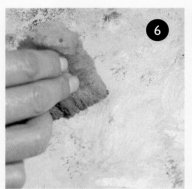

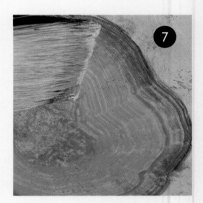

Photograph 5. With a soft cloth, lightly pat the ocher color evenly all over the surface of the pedestal.

Photograph 6. With the sponge, dab some areas with the brown paint.

Photograph 7. With a flat brush, create the veining characteristic of St Remy marble, using ocher, black, and white.

Photograph 8. Sponge these areas once more, but this time use the iron-oxide red.

Photograph 9. On top of the red paint, sponge patches of the ocher once more.

Photograph 10. Do the same with the dark brown.

Photograph 11. Apply the red once more to those areas you want to define. Note: the sponging has to be done before any of the colors dry.

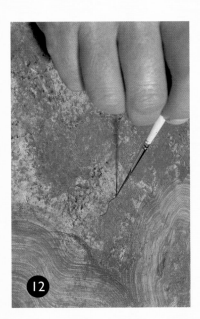

Photograph 12. With a fine artist's brush, stroke in the veins of the marble in a brown color; the unevenness of freehand painting can create a very realistic effect .

89

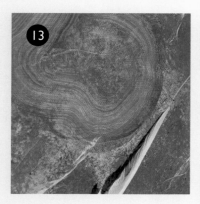

Photograph 13. Dip the bird's feather in white paint and stroke in the veins using the edge of the feather.

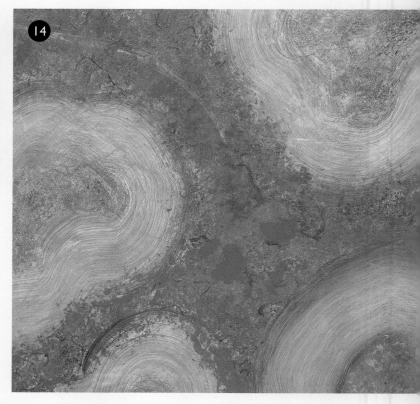

Photograph 14. Detail of the pedestal with the finished marble effect.

Photograph 15. Paint the moldings of the pedestal with a light gray paint.

Photograph 16. Once the paint has dried, apply a white glaze.

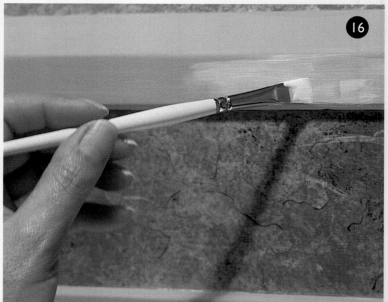

Photograph 17. Wipe off any excess glaze with a soft cloth and let it dry completely.

Photograph 18. Detail of the foot of the pedestal.

Photograph 19. The finished pedestal. The resemblance to the real thing can be very convincing.

14 Sponging

STEP BY STEP

WITH THIS TECHNIQUE YOU WILL ACHIEVE A LOOK THAT IS BOTH ORIGINAL AND OF A PROFESSIONAL QUALITY. IT IS WIDELY USED AND VERY POPULAR WITH BEGINNERS BECAUSE OF ITS SIMPLICITY AND ITS VERY ATTRACTIVE FINISH. IT CAN BE USED ON FURNITURE, TOYS, WALLS, IN CHILDREN'S BEDROOMS, KITCHENS, ETC. THE BASIC TOOL FOR THIS TECHNIQUE IS THE NATURAL SEA SPONGE, WITH WHICH A VERY THIN COAT OF PAINT IS DABBED OVER A VERY DIFFERENT (PREVIOUSLY PAINTED) COLOR.

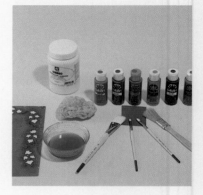

You will need:

Gesso, sandpaper, natural sponge, stencil with an ivy design, Gold Sable flat brush (No. 7), synthetic brush (No. 8), fine synthetic brush, stencil brush, acrylic colors (terracotta, red, vanilla, dark green, white, dark gray, and dark brown), satin varnish.

1

Photograph 1. For this example we have used a doll's house.

Photograph 2. Sand the entire surface of the house.

Photograph 3. Apply a coat of gesso to the whole area of the house and let it dry.

Photograph 4. Once the gesso has dried, sand the house again.

93

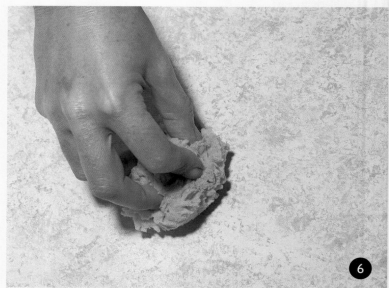

Photograph 5. We have chosen a very pale vanilla to use as the overall color. Paint the whole of the house, except for the windows and the roof. Before going on to next stage, let the paint dry completely.

Photograph 6. Dip the natural sponge into a darker color and sponge it on lightly over the vanilla. This is the sponging. Let it dry.

Photograph 7. Paint the roof of the house in a terracotta color to simulate roof tiles.

94

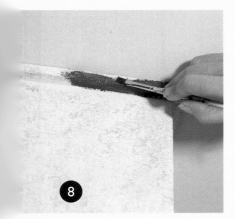

Photograph 8. The base of the house is painted in green to represent grass.

Photograph 9. Paint the windows in white and let the paint dry.

Photograph 10. With a stencil brush, paint the tree on the façade of the house. Use any green you like.

Photograph 11. With the help of a stencil, paint ivy creeping up and around the walls of the house. Use at least two different shades of green for this motif.

Photograph 12. Varnish the whole house with a satin varnish. Let it dry and sand down with sandpaper. Apply a second coat of varnish and wait until it dries.

Photograph 13. Detail of the lower part of the façade.

Photograph 14. The finished house. It could easily be used to house CDs rather than children's toys.

15

Central European style

STEP BY STEP

TRADITIONAL WARDROBES FROM THE TYROL AND FURNITURE FROM CENTRAL EUROPE ARE OFTEN DECORATED WITH MOTIFS THAT GIVE THEM AN ATTRACTIVE RICHNESS AND A VARIETY OF DETAIL AND COLOR. THE GENERAL LINE MUST BE ASYMMETRIC. THE CONTOURS AND MOLDINGS ARE PAINTED WITH TRADITIONAL COLORS. THE OVERALL DECORATION OF THESE PIECES OF FURNITURE GIVES THEM AN AGED LOOK. TO OBTAIN THIS, A SUITABLE PATINA MUST BE USED.

You will need:

Round brush (No. 3), fine brush, synthetic flat brushes (Nos. 8 and 10), Gold Sable flat brush (No. 7), pencil, gesso, yellow carbon-copy paper, tracing paper, tack cloth, bird's feather, sandpaper, natural sponge, masking tape, cloth, dark oak tint, antiquing, palette, polyurethane varnish, and acrylic colors (black, terracotta, yellow, white, beige, red, brown, umber, blue, and two different shades of green).

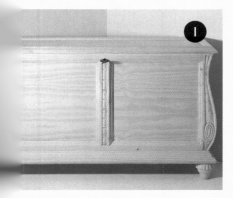

Photograph 1. The untreated chest in bare wood.

Photograph 2. Sand the entire surface of the chest.

Photograph 3. Apply a coat of gesso to those parts of the chest that are going to be painted.

Photograph 4. Apply the oak tint to the rest of the chest, including its interior.

Photograph 5. Before the tint dries, wipe off the excess with a cloth to prevent the forming of uneven patches.

Photograph 6. Sand the parts where the gesso was applied so that a dark green paint can then be applied at a later stage.

Photograph 7. With the yellow carbon-copy paper, transfer the design to the already dried panels. Use the masking tape to secure the paper.

Photograph 8. Detail of the design after it has been transferred. We chose a floral motif.

Photograph 9. With a fine artist's brush, paint the leaves in a lighter green.

Photograph 10. Paint the flowers (we have painted the roses in red) and the rest of the design.

Photograph 11. Paint the moldings of the panels in terracotta.

Photograph 12. The upper and lower moldings are painted in a different color. We have used black as a base so that we will be able to apply the marbling technique afterwards.

Photograph 13. Dip a natural sponge into different shades of paint and sponge over the already dried black areas. This will create an attractive effect.

Photograph 14. Dip the bird's feather in the white paint and, using the edge of the feather, imitate the veining of the marble over the sponging. Slide the feather across the surface lightly.

Photograph 15. Once this has dried, apply a coat of dark antiquing over the entire chest.

Photograph 16. With a cloth, rub the surface while the antiquing is still wet.

Photograph 17. Later, varnish the whole surface of the chest.

Photograph 18. A detail of one of the panels.

Photograph 19. The end result: a chest decorated in Central European style. The effect can be very imposing.

16

STEP BY STEP

Spattering

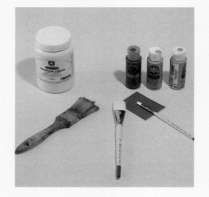

You will need:
Gesso, sandpaper, an old flat brush for spattering, fine synthetic brush, synthetic flat brush (No. 8), acrylic varnish, and acrylic colors (blue, beige, and gold).

THIS TECHNIQUE PRODUCES AN EFFECT IN WHICH SMALL DOTS OF COLOR ARE SPATTERED ALL OVER A SURFACE. IT'S ACHIEVED BY TAKING UP SOME COLORED VARNISH WITH A STIFF BRISTLE BRUSH (OR TOOTHBRUSH), AND THEN RUNNING A FINGER OR STICK ACROSS THE BRISTLES TO FLICK THE PAINT ONTO THE DECORATED SURFACE. THE EFFECT IS INTERESTINGLY VARIED, ESPECIALLY IF IT IS COMBINED WITH OTHER TECHNIQUES. THE COLORS CHOSEN FOR THE BASE AND THE SPATTERING MUST COMPLEMENT EACH OTHER. BEFORE YOU START ON A PIECE OF FURNITURE, IT'S ADVISABLE TO TRY THIS TECHNIQUE FIRST ON A PIECE OF WOOD OR CARD.

General view of the bookshelf that we will decorate.

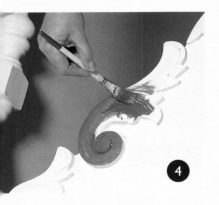

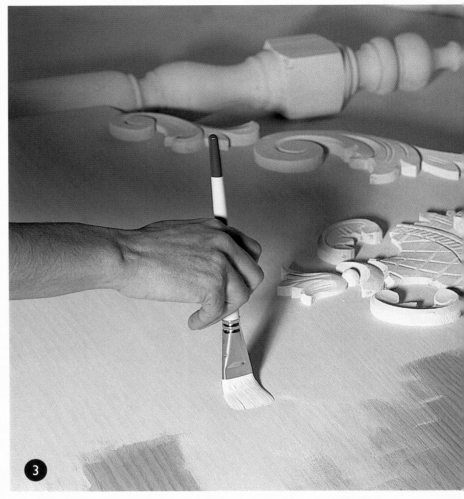

Photograph 2. Sand the entire surface to avoid any roughness in the wood.

Photograph 3. Apply three coats of gesso to the entire surface of the headboard.

Photograph 4. With a suitable red color, paint the moldings or any area where the gold foil is going to be applied.

Photograph 5. Once this has dried, apply a coat of adhesive to the same areas: this will stick the gold foil to the surface.

Photograph 6. With the help of a brush, apply the foil to the parts that have been covered with adhesive, making sure you fill all the crevices.

Photograph 7. Once the foil has dried, wipe away any loose foil.

Photograph 8. With the stipple brush, apply a blue glaze to the rest of the headboard by tapping the surface with the brush.

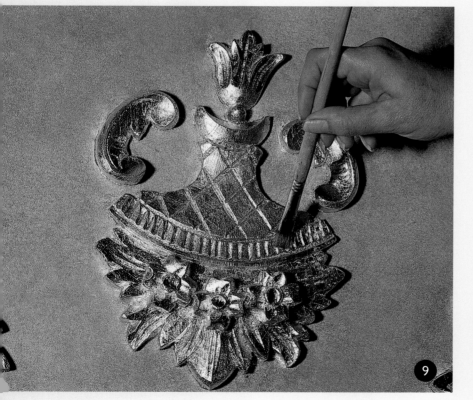

Photograph 9. Apply the sealer to all the areas where the foil has been applied.

Photograph 10. Brush on the antiquing, making sure you get into the crevices; once this has dried, apply another coat of sealer to protect the gold foil.

Photograph 11. Apply the first coat of acrylic varnish to the areas in blue; let it dry, and then apply two more coats.

Photograph 12. The finished headboard.

Photograph 12a. Detail of the central part of the headboard, decorated with the gold foil.

18 Oak root

STEP BY STEP

OAK ROOTS – FROM WHICH A VERY DISTINCTIVE WOOD IS EXTRACTED – ARE CHARACTERIZED BY THEIR GRAIN AND KNOTS. THE DIFFERENT SHADES, THE GRAINS, AND THE POSITION OF THE KNOTS, DEPEND ON WHERE EXACTLY AMONG THE ROOTS THE WOOD COMES FROM. THE TECHNIQUE WE USE IS THE SAME FOR ALL TYPES OF OAK ROOTS; THE ONLY THINGS THAT VARY ARE THE COLORS AND THE POSITION OF THE KNOTS. THIS TECHNIQUE IS VERY DECORATIVE AND CAN BE APPLIED TO SIMPLE, RUSTIC PIECES OF FURNITURE.

You will need:

Flat brush (No. 7), old flat brush, synthetic brush, softener brush, tack cloth, natural sponge, cloth, sandpaper, gesso, masking tape, thinner, light oak tint, gloss polyurethane varnish, and oil paints (sienna, ocher, and raw umber).

Photograph 1. In this example we have used a grandfather clock.

Photograph 2. Sand the entire area of the clock to eliminate any roughness.

Photograph 3. Apply a coat of gesso to those areas where the oak-root effect is going to be created.

Photograph 4. When the gesso has dried, sand it down to a smooth surface.

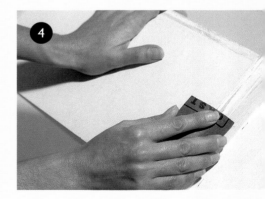

Photograph 5. Then apply a second coat of gesso.

Photograph 6. When dry, sand down once more.

Photograph 7. It's time for the oil paints. First, apply wide brush strokes of sienna.

Photograph 8. Next, apply the ocher near the sienna but not touching it.

Photograph 9. Finally, apply the raw umber over the other colors.

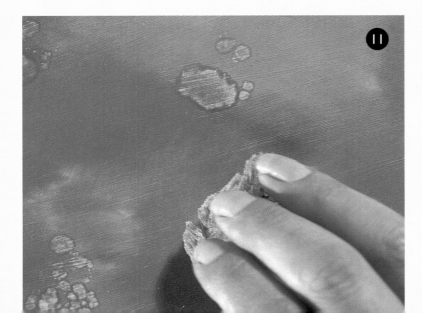

Photograph 12. Draw a folded cloth over the paint to create the effect of a wood grain.

Photograph 10. With a softener brush, blend all the colors.

Photograph 11. Before the paint dries, soak a sponge in thinner and touch it gently and randomly over the colors. The patches formed will gradually spread and form irregular shapes.

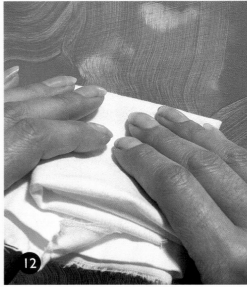

Photograph 13. The knots are imitated with a brush impregnated in raw umber color. A circular movement of the brush will create the knots.

Photograph 14. While the paints are still wet, blend the colors with a softener brush. They will take about a week to dry.

Photograph 15. The interior of the clock is stained in a light oak tint.

Photograph 16. Before the tint dries, wipe off any excess with a cloth.

Photograph 17. The moldings on the exterior are also stained with light oak tint. Allow it to dry.

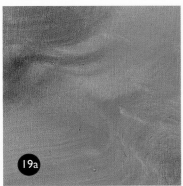

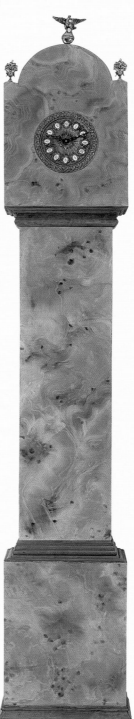

Photograph 18. Apply a coat of polyurethane varnish and let it dry. Sand between the second and third coat of varnish.

Photograph 19a. Detail of the clock that shows the imitation grain and the knots.

Photograph 19. In this photograph, we can appreciate the beautiful finish created with this technique.

19

STEP BY STEP

Drawing with a stylus

You will need:
India ink, stylus, black carbon-copy paper, tracing paper, sandpaper, synthetic flat brush (No. 8), flat brush (No. 7), fine brush, pencil, steel wool, light oak stain, and satin polyurethane varnish.

WITH THIS TRADITIONAL TECHNIQUE A STRIKING CONTRAST IS CREATED BETWEEN THE FINE AND DELICATE GRAINING OF CERTAIN WOODS AND A BOLD DECORATIVE DESIGN DRAWN WITH AN OPAQUE INK. THE MOST COMMONLY USED INKS ARE INDIA INK (BLACK) AND SEPIA (WARM BROWN). THIS PROCESS SEEMS SLOW AND FIDDLY, BUT ONCE THE DESIGN HAS BEEN TRANSFERRED AND THE PAINT HAS DRIED, THE PROCESS IS PRETTY QUICK. IT CONSISTS OF LIGHTLY MARKING THE CONTOURS OF A DESIGN ON A WOOD SURFACE AND THEN DRAWING THEM IN INK, WHICH IS APPLIED WITH A STYLUS OR AN ARTIST'S BRUSH. THIS FINISH IS IDEAL FOR LIGHT WOODS AS IT CREATES A STRONG CONTRAST. IT IS IMPORTANT TO SEAL THE WOOD BEFOREHAND.

Photograph 1. The table before being decorated.

1

Photograph 2. Sand the whole table to prepare the surface.

Photograph 3. With a light oak tint, stain the entire surface of the table, including the drawer.

Photograph 4. Once the tint has dried, smooth the entire surface with steel wool.

119

Photograph 5. Transfer the chosen design onto the top of the table and the lower shelf.

Photograph 6. Mark out the design with the help of the stylus and the India ink.

Photograph 7. With the same ink, but this time with a fine brush, paint the edges of the table.

Photograph 8. Once all the paint has dried, apply a coat of satin polyurethane varnish to the entire table. When it dries, apply another two coats of varnish.

Photograph 9a. Detail of the lower part of the table.

Photograph 9b. Detail of the upper part of the table. Here the hard work done with the stylus can be seen.

Photograph 9. General view of the finished table.

Y STEP

Large furniture

20 Dragging

STEP BY STEP

You will need:

Dragger, fine brush, Gold Sable flat brush (No. 6), round brush (No. 3), sandpaper, flogger, palette, tracing paper, black carbon-copy paper, gesso, acrylic varnish, white glaze and acrylic colors (white, red, yellow, light green, medium blue, pastel pink, green, and a strong blue).

THIS TECHNIQUE EMULATES THE NATURAL GRAIN OF WOOD. IN THE PAST, DRAGGING WAS USED TO DECORATE WALLS, ESPECIALLY IN THE SPACE BETWEEN THE CEILING AND THE PICTURE RAIL; THE OTHER AREAS OF THE WALL WERE USUALLY COVERED WITH A MARBLE OR STIPPLE EFFECT. DRAGGING PRODUCES SOFT GROOVES; A SPECIAL BRUSH CALLED A DRAGGER OR FLOGGER IS USED TO CREATE THIS FINISH. NOTE: IT'S ALWAYS BETTER TO FOLLOW THE GRAIN OF THE WOOD.

View of the cot we decorated.

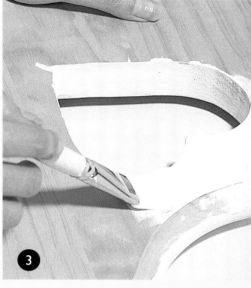

Photograph 1. The cot before work began on it.

Photograph 2. To prepare the surfaces, sand down the entire cot.

Photograph 3. Apply a coat of gesso to the whole cot and, when it has dried, sand it all down.

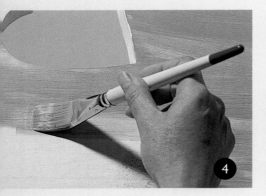

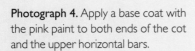

Photograph 4. Apply a base coat with the pink paint to both ends of the cot and the upper horizontal bars.

Photograph 5. With the flogger, apply white glaze to both ends of the cot. Drag the flogger carefully from one end to the other in one clean sweep; this will create the required streaked effect.

Photograph 6. With the black carbon-copy paper, trace your design onto the parts where the glaze has just been applied.

Photograph 7. Paint the design. The colors chosen depend on each person's individual taste.

Photograph 8. Paint the edges of the ends of the cot and the vertical bars of the sides with a flat brush.

Photograph 9. Varnish the entire cot with synthetic varnish. This type of varnish is non-toxic – we are, of course, decorating a child's cot.

Photograph 10. This photograph reveals the full effect of the painting.

Photographs 11 and 12. Details of the designs used at both ends of the cot. On one end there is a tied ribbon; on the other, two rabbits and a ribbon.

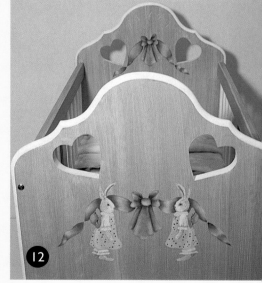

127

21

STEP BY STEP

Crackled finish

You will need:
Synthetic fine brush, synthetic flat brush (No. 7), stencil brush, cloth, sandpaper, masking tape, oak-brown tint, gesso, crackle varnish, stencil, polyurethane matt varnish, and acrylic colors (ocher and blue-green).

IN THIS TECHNIQUE A SPECIAL VARNISH MUST BE USED: AS THIS CLEAR VARNISH DRIES, ITS SURFACE CRACKS, PRODUCING THE EFFECT OF TIME AND OLD AGE. IT'S A GOOD IDEA TO COMBINE THIS VARNISH WITH AN ANTIQUING MEDIUM OR GEL. THE SURFACE MUST NOT BE POROUS, OTHERWISE IT WILL ABSORB THE FIRST COAT OF VARNISH AND CRACKS WILL NOT APPEAR. THE LONGER THE TIME BETWEEN APPLYING COATS, THE FEWER THE CRACKS THAT WILL APPEAR.

The finished bottle rack that is featured in this section.

Photograph 1. The bottle rack before we applied the crackling technique.

Photograph 2. Sand the entire surface of the bottle rack.

Photograph 3. Apply a coat of gesso to those areas that are going to be covered with the crackled effect. Once it has dried, smooth it with sandpaper.

Photograph 4. Stain those parts of the bottle rack that are going to be crackled.

Photograph 5. Wipe away any excess tint before it dries.

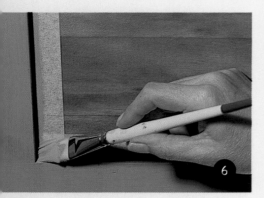

Photograph 6. Protect the stained areas with masking tape and proceed to paint with the ocher acrylic paint the parts where the gesso was applied.

Photograph 7. Once the ocher paint has dried, apply the crackle and then let it dry.

Photograph 8. On the same area, apply a blue-green paint.

Photograph 9. Once the blue-green paint has dried, the cracks become apparent and the ocher paint applied beforehand can be seen between the cracks.

Photograph 10. With the stencil, create a design on the sides of the bottle rack, on the drawers and the shelf, using the blue-green and ocher.

Photograph 11. When everything has dried, sand the design gently to give it a slightly worn, aged look.

Photograph 12. Apply a coat of polyurethane varnish, let it dry and repeat this process twice.

Photograph 13. The bottle rack after it has been decorated.

Photograph 13a. Detail of the design on the side of the bottle rack.

22

Italian style

STEP BY STEP

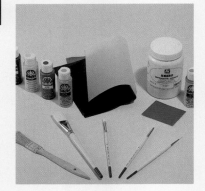

THE ITALIANS HAVE USED GESSO – WHICH IS IDEAL AS A BASE WHEN DECORATING FURNITURE – SINCE THE 15TH CENTURY. IT WAS FREQUENTLY USED AS A LIGHT BASE FOR VENETIAN AND FLORENTINE PIECES OF FURNITURE. NOWADAYS, GESSO IS USED TO GIVE GOLD LEAF AN AGED LOOK.

You will need:
Flat brush (No. 7), fine synthetic brush, round brushes (Nos. 2 and 4), sandpaper, gesso, tracing paper, black carbon-copy paper, and acrylic colors (silver, dark green, light green, gray, and light cream), polyurethane varnish.

The bureau that we decorated using the Italian style.

Photograph 1. The bureau before the technique was used.

Photograph 2. Sand the entire surface of the bureau to obtain a smooth finish.

Photograph 3. Apply a coat of gesso to the whole surface.

Photograph 4. When the gesso has dried, sand the surface once more.

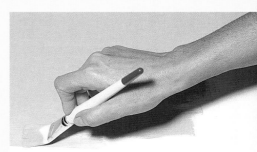

Photograph 5. Paint the entire surface of the bureau with the light green paint.

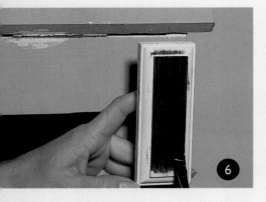

Photograph 6. Paint the edges of the drawers and the front of the supports for the top shelf (when opened) in the darker green.

Photograph 7. Apply the silver to the dark green.

Photograph 8. Once you have chosen the design, place it on the bureau and secure it with masking tape. Trace it on to the surface with the help of the carbon-copy paper.

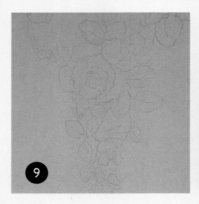

Photograph 9. Detail of the design.

Photograph 10. Paint the design in the light cream color; this should contrast effectively with the green.

Photograph 11. Trace the details of the design in another color. We have used dark gray.

Photograph 12. Finally, apply three coats of polyurethane varnish to the entire surface of the bureau.

Photograph 13. The finished bureau in all its glory.

Photograph 13a. Detail of the design.

23 Painting with vinegar

STEP BY STEP

You will need:
Honey-color tint, sandpaper, tack cloth, oil, straw scouring pad, wax, vinegar, acrylic paint (dark brown, white, and blue), flat brush, pencil, tracing paper, yellow carbon-copy paper, masking tape, steel wool, and polyurethane satin varnish.

THIS KIND OF PAINTING COULD BE DESCRIBED AS TYPICAL OF CENTRAL EUROPE. IT IS THE CHEAPEST WAY OF MAKING GLAZES, SINCE THE MATERIALS USED CAN BE FOUND IN ALMOST ANY HOUSEHOLD.

THE WAX BASE PREVENTS THE MIXTURE OF PAINT AND VINEGAR FROM DRYING OUT TOO QUICKLY, WHICH ALLOWS SUFFICIENT TIME TO COMPLETE THE FINISH.

This wardrobe is a superb piece of furniture, to be placed in a corner reserved for a very special piece.

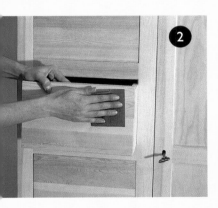

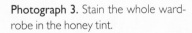

Photograph 1. The wardrobe in bare wood.

Photograph 2. Sand the entire surface of the wardrobe.

Photograph 3. Stain the whole wardrobe in the honey tint.

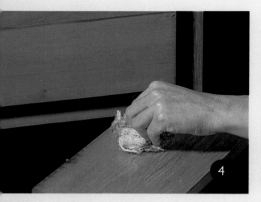

Photograph 4. Wipe off any excess tint with a cloth before it dries.

Photograph 5. Once the tint has dried, rub the whole surface with a straw scouring pad to soften it.

Photograph 6. Using a soft cloth, wax the whole wardrobe.

Photograph 7. Then apply a mixture made up with acrylic dark brown paint and vinegar.

Photograph 8. Before this mixture dries, make circular patterns with a brush all over the wardrobe.

Photograph 9. Trace the chosen design on the front of the drawer with the help of yellow carbon-copy paper. Secure the paper with masking tape.

Photograph 10. Do the same on the wardrobe's door.

Photograph 11. Detail of the design on the wardrobe's door.

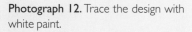

Photograph 12. Trace the design with white paint.

Photograph 13. Make use of the masking tape to define where the blue color is going to go.

Photograph 14. With the white paint, apply a few strokes inside the design.

Photograph 15. Varnish the whole wardrobe with polyurethane varnish.

Photograph 16. Once the varnish has dried, apply a coat of wax to the entire wardrobe with steel wool. Then buff the surface with a cotton cloth to obtain a fine luster.

Photograph 17. The finished wardrobe. The floral designs on the door and the drawer can be seen here, as well as the circles that have been created with the vinegar.

141

24 Liming

STEP BY STEP

THIS TECHNIQUE IS GENERALLY USED ON WOODS WITH VERY OPEN GRAIN. THE PORES OF THE WOOD ARE COVERED WITH A SPECIAL PASTE THAT ENHANCES THE PATTERN OF THE GRAIN. IF YOU WANT TO STAIN THE PASTE, MAKE SURE THAT THE TINT IS NOT TOO DARK, AS MOST OF THE COLORS USED ARE PASTEL SHADES.

You will need:

Two old flat brushes (No. 8), two round brushes (Nos. 5 and 2), pencil, tracing paper, sandpaper, white (liming) wax, tack cloth, sealer, masking tape, medium oak tint, tracing paper, oil-based varnish, yellow carbon-copy paper, vinegar, and acrylic colors (white and blue).

The full effect of this technique can readily be seen in this photograph of the washstand we decorated.

Photograph 1. A full view of the antique washstand before applying this technique.

Photograph 2. Sand down the whole washstand.

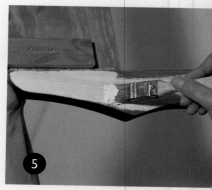

Photograph 3. Apply a medium oak tint to enhance the color of the wood.

Photograph 5. Next, apply a coat of white wax (liming wax) to the entire washstand.

Photograph 4. Once the tint has dried, apply a coat of sealer.

144

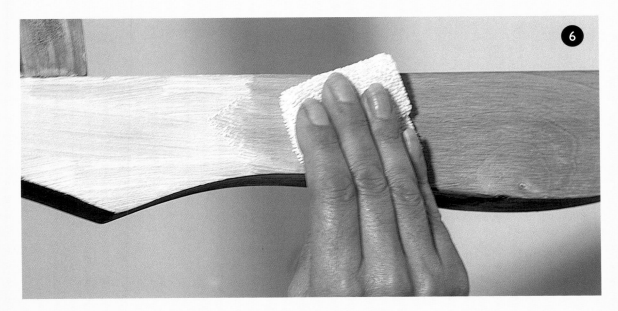

Photograph 6. With a soft cloth, wipe away the residue of the wax.

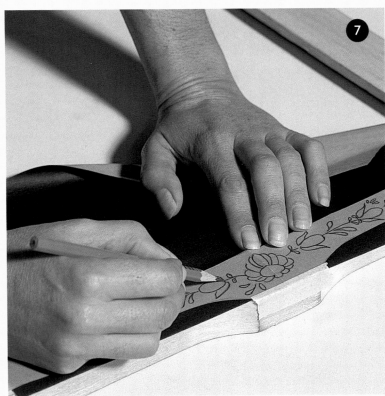

Photograph 7. Trace the design onto the wood with the help of yellow carbon-copy paper. Secure it with masking tape.

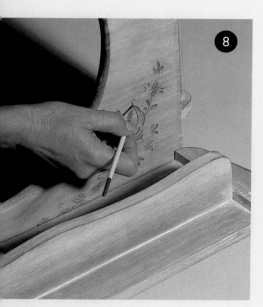

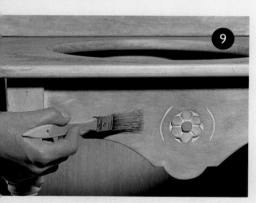

Photograph 10. This photograph reveals the overall effect of the liming technique.

Photograph 8. Paint the design you have traced.

Photograph 9. Apply a first coat of oil-based varnish and let it dry. Repeat two more times.

Photograph 11a. Detail of the design on the front.

Photograph 11b. As you can see in this photograph, the jug has been decorated with the same colors as the washstand.

Photograph 11. The finished look of the washstand with accessories.

25

STEP BY STEP

Distressed look

You will need:
Old keys, screws, a set of screwdrivers, hammer, two flat brushes (No. 7) sandpaper, steel wool, tack cloth, straw scouring pad, dark cherry tint, beeswax, and sealer.

"DISTRESSING" TECHNIQUES ARE USED TO GIVE NEW FURNITURE AN OLD, EVEN ANTIQUE, LOOK. THE SIMPLEST WAY TO ACHIEVE THIS IS TO OBSERVE FURNITURE FROM THE PERIOD YOU WISH TO REPRODUCE AND TRY TO IMITATE ITS CHARACTERISTICS. THIS TYPE OF WORK IS MORE SUITABLE FOR RESTORING FURNITURE THAN IT IS FOR DECORATING IT.

NEVERTHELESS, WITHIN THE LATEST RESTORATION TECHNIQUES THERE IS ONE, BASED ON THE PREPARATION OF SURFACES, THAT CAN ACCOMPLISH A CONVINCING ANTIQUE LOOK. IT CONSISTS OF DAMAGING – DISTRESSING – THE SURFACE THAT YOU ARE GOING TO WORK ON INSTEAD OF RESTORING IT.

The distressed look gives this piece of furniture an antique appearance.

Photograph 1. The dresser before treatment.

Photograph 2. Sand down the entire piece.

Photograph 3. Apply the beeswax with steel wool.

153

Photograph 4. Apply the blue paint that you have chosen before the wax is fully absorbed. Because of the wax, the blue paint will not cover the dresser completely. Paint the lilac areas.

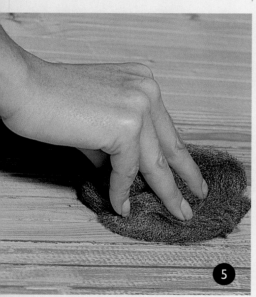

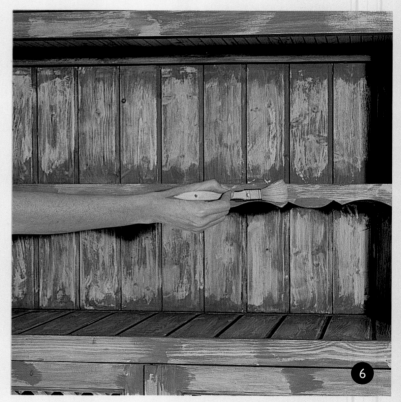

Photograph 5. Once the paint has dried, rub the entire surface with the steel wool.

Photograph 6. Apply the first coat of polyurethane varnish and let it dry. Apply a second coat of varnish, let it dry and then apply a third coat.

154

Photograph 7. The finished dresser.

Photograph 7a. Detail of the central part of the dresser where the application of the two colors can be seen.

27 Painting with feathers

STEP BY STEP

THIS TECHNIQUE IS A VARIATION OF MARBLING ON WOOD. THE TECHNIQUE OF FLOGGING CREATES A MORE UNIFORM FINISH – FEATHERS PRODUCE AN UNEVEN AND INFORMAL FINISH. ANY TYPE OF FEATHER THAT IS STRONG, LONG, AND FLEXIBLE CAN BE USED, SUCH AS A PHEASANT OR PEACOCK FEATHER.

You will need:
Sandpaper, synthetic flat brushes (Nos. 7 and 8), gesso, acrylic varnish, medium oak tint, glaze, some long feathers, tack cloth, and acrylic paints (blue and ocher).

The finished chiffonier.

Photograph 1. The chiffonier before work began.

Photograph 2. Sand the entire piece, including the drawers.

Photograph 3. Apply gesso to all the external parts and let it dry thoroughly.

Photograph 4. Sand down the gesso to a smooth surface.

Photograph 5. Apply another coat of gesso, and when that has dried repeat the sanding.

Photograph 6. Stain the interior of the drawer with the oak tint.

Photograph 7. Wipe off the excess tint with a cloth.

Photograph 8. With the chosen ocher color, paint the exterior of the chiffonier and let it dry.

Photograph 9. Apply a blue glaze to the entire surface.

Photograph 10. "Flog" the glaze with a bunch of feathers while the glaze is still wet.

Photograph 11. Paint the columns and the handles with the blue acrylic paint.

Photograph 12. A detail of the columns.

Photograph 13. Apply acrylic varnish to the entire chiffonier. Once it has dried, repeat this step twice.

Photograph 14. The chiffonier after it has been decorated.

Photograph 14a. Detail of the chiffonier; here the effect created with the feathers can clearly be seen.

28 Glazing

STEP BY STEP

You will need:
Flat brush (No. 7), synthetic fine brush, sandpaper, glaze, glue gun, stapler, cloth, brown braid, material for upholstery, gesso, polyurethane varnish, and acrylic gold paint.

IN DECORATIVE TECHNIQUES, GLAZE IS A TRANSLUCENT PAINT GENERALLY USED OVER A CONTRASTING BASE COLOR. IN THE EXAMPLE WE WILL WORK ON, A STOOL IS SANDED UNTIL ALL PREVIOUS VARNISH HAS BEEN REMOVED AND THE WOOD STARTS TO LOOK NEW. THE GLAZE WILL GIVE THIS PIECE OF FURNITURE A COMPLETELY DIFFERENT APPEARANCE AND COLOR. THE APPLICATION OF GOLD PAINT IN SPECIFIC AREAS WILL ENHANCE AN ANTIQUE LOOK.

The finished stool once the glaze paint has been applied.

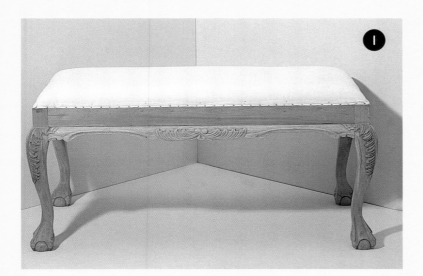

Photograph 1. The stool in its prelimi-
nary stage.

Photograph 2. Sand the entire piece.

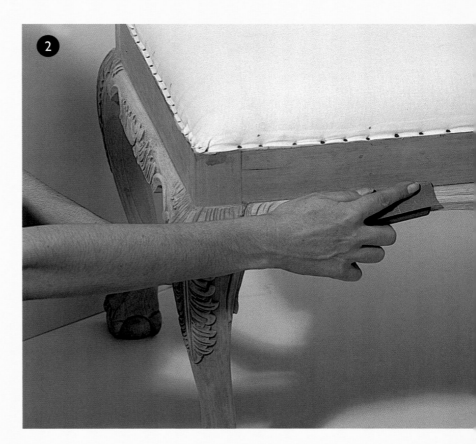

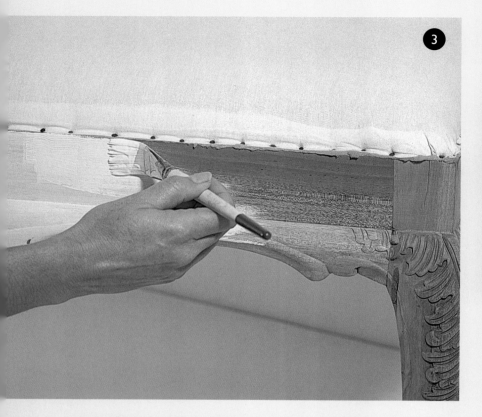

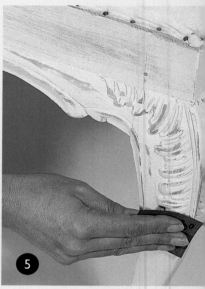

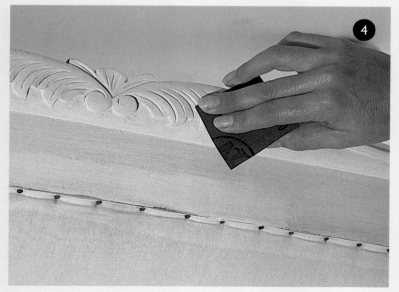

Photograph 3. Apply a coat of gesso to all the wooden areas.

Photograph 4. Once the gesso has dried, sand it down vigorously…

Photograph 5. … but this time only in the prominent areas. The aim is to allow the bare wood to show through.

Photograph 6. With a brush, apply a coat of green glaze to all the wood.

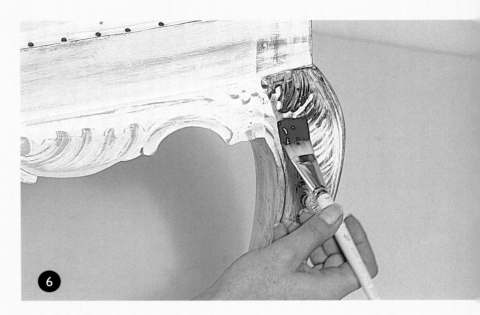

Photograph 7. Use a cloth to wipe away any excess glaze before it dries.

Photograph 8. On those areas that were sanded twice, apply a coat of gold paint with your finger.

Photograph 9. Once the gold paint has dried, apply a coat of polyurethane varnish and let it dry. Apply a second coat of varnish.

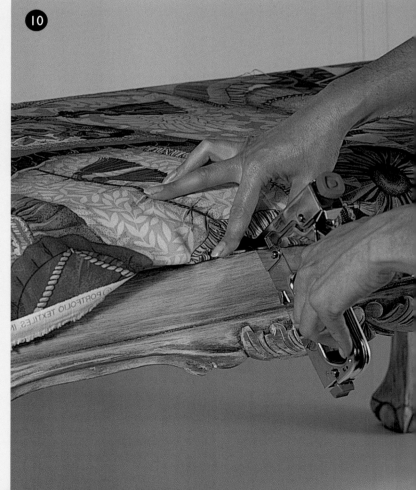

Photograph 10. Cover the seat of the stool with the selected material. The stapler will help you to do this job.

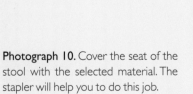

Photograph 11. Glue the braid over the staples and secure it by applying hot glue with a glue gun.

Photograph 12. The stool is ready to be used and admired.

Photograph 12a. Detail of the material we have chosen for the seat of the stool.

29 Ragging

STEP BY STEP

THIS TECHNIQUE DOES NOT USE COLORED EMULSION. INSTEAD, THINNED PAINT IS USED TO PARTIALLY COVER THE PREVIOUS COAT. THEN THE WET PAINT IS LIFTED OFF WITH A PIECE OF CRUNCHED-UP POLYTHENE (OR OTHER MATERIAL), CREATING A PICTURESQUE RANDOM EFFECT.

You will need:
Flat brush (No. 7), sandpaper, small synthetic brush, polythene (or cloth or cellophane), gesso, artist's gel thickener, polyurethane varnish, and acrylic colors from Folkart (red 827 and black 925).

The glass cabinet we decorated.

Photograph 1. The glass cabinet in bare wood.

Photograph 2. Sand the entire surface smooth.

Photograph 3. Apply a coat of gesso.

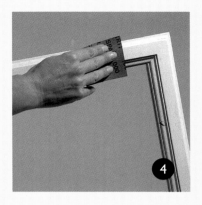

Photograph 4. Wait until it has dried and then sand it down.

Photograph 5. Apply a base coat in red paint (acrylic) and let it dry.

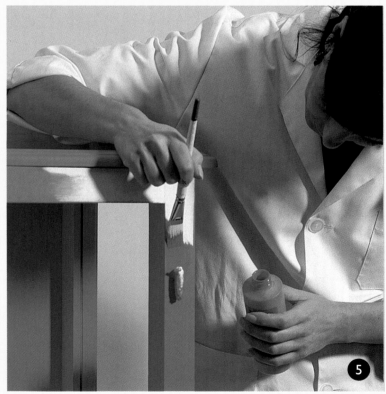

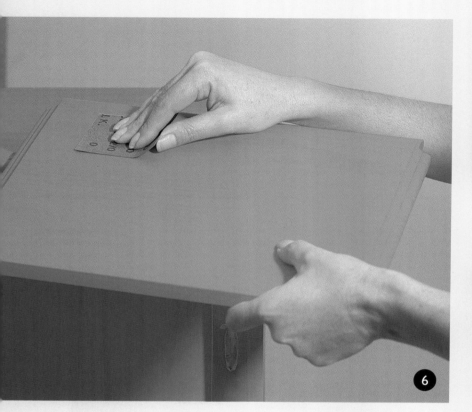

Photograph 6. Once the paint has dried, sand the entire piece to produce a smooth surface.

Photograph 7. Apply a coat of black glaze over the red paint.

Photograph 8. Before the glaze dries, press a piece of crunched-up polythene (or cellophane or cloth) over the base of the glass cabinet to create distinctive patterns. These will depend on the material you use, how tightly you crumple it, and how exactly you apply it to the surface.

Photograph 9. Once the glaze is dry, apply a coat of polyurethane varnish to the entire glass cabinet.

Photograph 12. The beautiful and highly individual finish achieved with this technique can be seen in this photograph.

Photographs 10 and 11. Details of the different parts of the glass cabinet.

30 Painting with liquid masking

STEP BY STEP

THIS TECHNIQUE IS BASED ON THE FACT THAT LIQUID MASKING CAN BE USED TO SEAL AREAS ON A PAINTED SURFACE. A DESIGN CAN BE DRAWN WITH LIQUID MASKING AND PAINTED OVER – THE MASKING LIQUID, WHICH DRIES TO A RUBBERY CONSISTENCY, FORMS A WATERPROOF FILM THAT THE PAINT CANNOT PENETRATE. THIS TECHNIQUE IS IDEAL FOR DECORATING WOOD WITH AN EVEN GRAIN, SUCH AS PINE, OAK, OR ASH.

You will need:

Paintbrush (No. 7), ox's ear's fine brush (No. 3), sandpaper, eraser, tracing paper, black carbon-copy paper, liquid masking, tack cloth, masking tape, polyurethane varnish, and navy blue and orange tint.

The lamp stand we decorated with this technique.

Photograph 1. The lamp stand in bare wood.

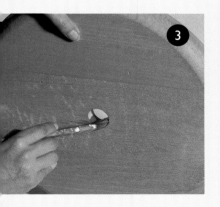

Photograph 2. Sand the whole surface of the lamp stand.

Photograph 3. Stain the entire surface with the orange tint.

Photograph 4. Wipe off any excess tint with a cloth.

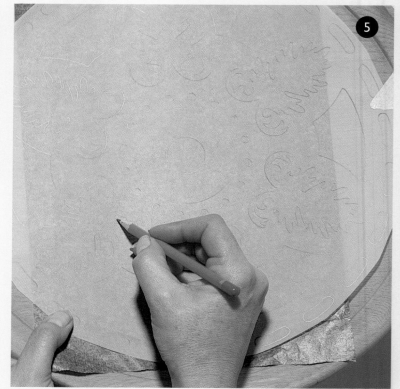

Photograph 5. Transfer your chosen design to the base of the lamp stand and trace it using the carbon-copy paper. Do the same on the foot of the lamp. (We have used a different design for the foot.)

Photograph 6. Cover those areas that you want to keep orange with liquid masking to protect them from other colors used. The liquid masking will act as a shield.

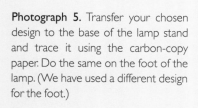

Photograph 7. Apply a blue tint to the tray. Define the center with masking tape; this area will be painted later in another color. In this case we have used the orange color.

174

Photograph 8. Wipe away any excess blue tint with a cloth.

Photograph 9. Once the tint has dried, rub off the liquid masking with an eraser to allow the orange color to show through the blue.

Photograph 10. Varnish the entire piece with polyurethane varnish and let it dry. Varnish two more times.

Photograph 11. The finished lamp stand. Here the bright combination of the two colors can be appreciated.